SECOND • EDITION

SEAFOOD

A Collection Of Heart-Healthy Recipes

Other books by Janis Harsila, R.D. and Evie Hansen
Light-Hearted Seafood

Other books authored by Janis Harsila, R.D. or Evie Hansen
Selling Seafood
Seafood Treasures

Design and illustrations by Martine Richards Fabrizio
Typesetting and production by
Technigraphic Systems, Inc. – Edmonds, Washington
Editor – Diane Baker
Printing by Bookcrafters – Chelsea, Michigan
Cover photo – Kodiak Seafood, Seattle, Washington
Steve Bonini Photography, Portland, Oregon

Special Thanks To:
Seafood Business
Cindy Welke Snyder, R.D. – Diabetic Exchanges
McKnight & Co., Inc.

PUBLISHED BY NATIONAL SEAFOOD EDUCATORS

Janis Harsila, R.D. and Evie Hansen

National Seafood Educators
Richmond Beach, Washington

Requests for such permission should be addressed to:

National Seafood Educators
P.O. Box 60006
Richmond Beach, WA 98160
(206) 546-6410

Printed and bound in the United States of America
Second Edition
Third Printing - October 1992

ISBN: 0-9616426-2-9

Library of Congress Catalog Number: 90-61209

Dedicated to our children,
Scott and Katie Harsila, and Mickey Hansen.

PREFACE

In its first edition, *Seafood: A Collection of Heart-Healthy Recipes* became a national best-seller. During the years since the book's publication, over and over, across the country, we have heard you say "we want to eat more seafood but we need to know more." People have so many questions about seafood ranging from how to buy top quality seafood to knowing when fish is cooked. Hearts are saying "eat more seafood", but hands don't know how to do it!

To continue to provide the information you want, we have completely revised and updated this book. This edition of *Seafood: A Collection of Heart-Healthy Recipes* tells everything about seafood - from A to Z. There are easy guidelines for proper seafood selection, home storage and preparation that make seafood buying and cooking a breeze. The "Ten Top Tips For Shopping For Seafood" is a quick and clear guide to selection at the seafood counter.

The book includes an expanded seafood nutrition information section and now has a weight loss guide and dieting tips. Medical research over the past decade has clearly identified the health benefits of eating seafood and seafood is the perfect choice for the calorie-conscious. New dieting tips help you to include seafood as part of any weight control program. Also, diabetic exchanges have now been added.

The recipes are nutritious, delicious and easy to prepare. Many recipes have been updated and new recipes have been added. We have included the latest seafood products on the market. Two new recipe chapters are: "Entertaining with Seafood" and "Romantic Dinners for Two".

Seafood is an important part of our own families' diets. We eat seafood several times a week. We want to share with you the tips we've discovered while shopping at the seafood counter and while cooking seafood in our own homes. We want to help you serve seafood more often! To your good health!

Janis Harsila, R.D.
Evie Hansen

TABLE OF CONTENTS

CHAPTER ONE

SEAFOOD FROM A TO Z

CHAPTER 1

SEAFOOD FROM A TO Z

HEALTH BENEFITS OF SEAFOOD

Seafood is the perfect food choice for calorie conscious individuals. It is low in calories and fat and has positive benefits for overall health, especially weight loss and heart health!

SEAFOOD IS:

- **Low in Calories.**
- **Low in Total Fat, Saturated Fat and Cholesterol.**
- **High in Polyunsaturated Fats and Omega-3 Fatty Acids.**
- **High in Protein.**
- **A Great Source of Vitamins and Minerals.**
- **Low in Sodium.**
- **Easily Chewed and Digested.**
- **Quick and Easy to Prepare.**

■ **Seafood is low in calories.** Seafood is perfect for weight loss or weight maintenance diets. An average 3½ ounce serving of seafood has less than 100 calories compared with beef at 200 calories. A 3½ ounce portion of cod, for example, has just 82 calories; an equal serving of oysters has a modest 70 calories. Seafood can even be easily and deliciously prepared with few added calories.

■ **Seafood is very low in total fat, saturated fat and cholesterol.** Sole, cod, shrimp and haddock all have less than one gram of fat per 3½ ounce serving. Cholesterol levels in seafood are low in most cases. Two seafood species with especially low cholesterol levels are mussels and albacore tuna, containing only 25 mgs. cholesterol per 3½ ounce serving!

The following table compares the percentage of calories that comes from fat in seafood to the percentage in other meat and poultry sources.

Percent Calories From Fat: Seafood Versus Other Meat Sources

3½ ounce, raw, edible portion	Calories	Fat (grams)	% Calories From Fat
Cod	82	0.7	8%
Shrimp	90	0.8	8%
Halibut	105	1.2	10%
Chicken breast, flesh without skin	110	1.3	11%
Oysters	70	1.2	15%
Rockfish, snapper	97	1.8	17%
Beef, eye of round, trimmed	131	4.3	30%
Pork, center loin chop, trimmed	159	7.2	41%
T-bone steak, short loin, trimmed	159	8.0	45%
Ground beef, very lean, broiled	238	14.2	54%
Beef, Chuck, ground, cooked	327	23.9	66%

Even the highest fat seafood is lower in fat than most meat sources! Virtually all seafood derives between 7% and 30% of its calories from fat. Comparing these levels with those of other animal protein sources, beef, pork, lamb and most varieties of chicken derive between 30% and 70% of their calories from fat!

■ **Seafood is high in polyunsaturated fats and omega-3 fatty acids.** Seafood's unique fat make-up plays an important role in its reported health benefits. A high proportion of fats in seafood are polyunsaturated fats, compared with fats in meat and poultry which are mainly saturated. Also, the polyunsaturated fats in seafood contain significant amounts of omega-3 fatty acids. In fact, omega-3 fatty acids are even more unsaturated than vegetable oils (a definite health advantage).

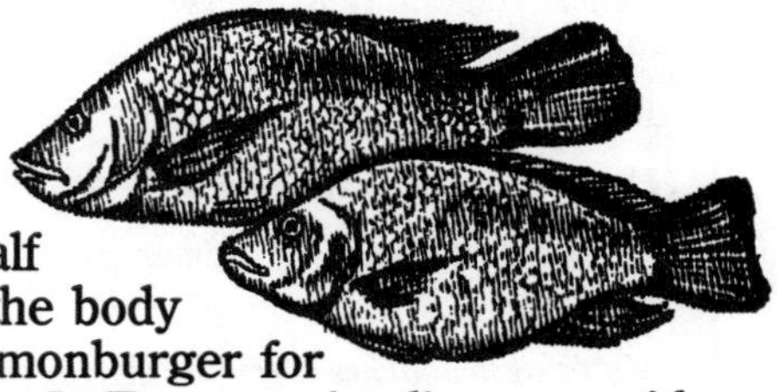

■ **Seafood is high in protein.** One 3½ ounce serving of seafood supplies about half the total protein required by the body each day. One example: a salmonburger for lunch and one serving of Halibut In Tarragon for dinner provide the day's total protein requirement for the average woman, with minimal calories and maximum flavor.

■ **Seafood is a great source of vitamins and minerals.** Seafood contains many of the vitamins and minerals that we need each day. Among them are thiamine, riboflavin, pantothenic acid, niacin, phosphorous, potassium, iron, iodine, fluoride, zinc, selenium and copper. For instance, clams, mussels and oysters are good sources of iron and zinc; canned salmon and sardines (with bones) contain high levels of calcium.

■ **Seafood is low in sodium.** Fresh seafood is one of the best choices for cutting back on sodium intake since most varieties are low in sodium.

■ **Seafood is easily chewed and digested.** Having less connective tissue than meat seafood is to chew and digest. Seafood is great for children and the elderly. We recommend boneless fish as a first protein choice for toddlers.

■ **Seafood is quick and easy to prepare.** Seafood is an original "fast food." Most seafood recipes, including all recipes in this book, can be prepared quickly and easily, usually within 15 to 20 minutes. This is a must for those of us with busy lifestyles!

OMEGA-3 FATTY ACID RESEARCH

The health benefits of eating seafood and, in particular, the benefits of omega-3 fatty acids have captured the attention of the scientific community. Research is very recent, only taking place during the past 20 years. Even though most research is still in early stages, outcomes look very promising.

Omega-3 fatty acids are thought to have positive effects on:

Cancer (especially breast, colon and prostate cancers);

Diabetes;

High blood pressure (mild lowering);

Psoriasis (decrease in redness and itching);

Migraine headaches (decrease in frequency and intensity);

Arthritis;

Auto-immune diseases (such as lupus erythematosus); and

Inflammatory diseases (decrease).

The most publicized area of research is omega-3 fatty acids' role in preventing coronary heart disease and their role in lowering blood triglyceride levels.

Scientists theorize that omega-3's counter atherosclerosis (hardening of the arteries) by inhibiting blood clotting. Blood becomes thinner and individual blood cells actually become less sticky and more slippery. This then leads to decreased formation of atherosclerotic plaques. These effects seem to be more important in preventing heart disease than seafood's effect on cholesterol levels.

Studies have clearly identified the positive role of omega-3 fatty acids in heart health. Other areas of promising research include the beneficial effect of omega-3 fatty acids on almost every other organ system and biochemical pathway in the body.

A word of caution about fish oil pills:

Health professionals recommend obtaining omega-3 fatty acids from seafood, not from fish oil pills. Studies have shown that consuming fish oil pills possibly may have adverse effects such as increasing blood LDL (a less desirable lipid) and blood sugar levels. Fish oil pills should only be taken when prescribed by a physician. It is safer, less expensive and more enjoyable to obtain omega-3 fatty acids from a meal of seafood!

Learning From The Greenland Eskimos

Some of the initial omega-3 fatty acid studies were done in the early 1970's when Greenland Eskimos were first recognized for their very low incidence of heart disease and also their general good health. Eskimos enjoy low cancer and diabetes rates, low blood levels of cholesterol and triglycerides, and high levels of healthy blood lipids. Scientists have attributed the Eskimo health profile to a diet consisting of large amounts of seafood products. The average Eskimo's diet consists of almost a pound a day of seafood products.

However, we don't need to eat a pound of fish per day to attain health benefits from eating seafood! Studies have shown that as little as **seven ounces of seafood per week** can help prevent heart disease! *The New England Journal of Medicine* (May 1985) recommends:

"One to two fish dishes a week in dietary guidelines for the prevention of coronary heart disease."

The media and scientific communities often report that we should eat high fat fish, such as salmon, mackerel and herring, because of their high levels of omega-3 fatty acids. However, **all seafood contains omega-3 fatty acids.** Fattier seafoods such as salmon, mackerel and herring do have more total omega-3 fatty acids than leaner seafood such as cod. **But**, in low fat seafoods, the concentration of omega-3 fatty acids in the fat is actually greater. It is important to remember to eat a wide variety of seafood, high fat and low fat. You are receiving omega-3's no matter what seafood you eat!

The following table compares the total fat and the amount of omega-3 fatty acids to the concentration of omega-3 fatty acids in the fat.

100 grams, raw, edible portion	Total fat (grams)	Omega-3 fatty acids (grams)	Omega 3 fatty acids % of total fat
Shrimp	0.8	0.3	37%
Cod	0.6	0.2	33%
Herring	8.5	1.7	20%
Salmon, Sockeye	8.6	1.2	14%

THE SHELLFISH CONTROVERSY

There is a great deal of misunderstanding among consumers and even health professionals about shellfish and whether it is heart-healthy. We all know fish is good for us. But does that include shellfish, too? The answer is an emphatic yes! Shellfish is high in protein and low in fat (only 1-3% fat). It is low in calories, sodium and saturated fats, and high in polyunsaturated fats. Omega-3 fatty acids also make up a substantial portion of the fat content.

In the past, scientists reported that shellfish had high amounts of cholesterol. However, technology was crude and could not distinguish cholesterol from non-cholesterol sterols which appeared chemically to be the same. It has been determined that, for virtually all species of shellfish, cholesterol is only part of the total sterol content. The total sterol content includes cholesterol as well as a variety of non-cholesterol sterols which have no effect on blood cholesterol levels. Non-cholesterol sterols can account for up to 70% of the total sterol content in shellfish.

Further good news is that these non-cholesterol sterols are poorly absorbed by the body and they also appear to interfere with the absorption of cholesterol. Because of this, much of the cholesterol does not even get into the blood stream. What a bonus!

Shellfish are divided into two categories: crustaceans and mollusks. Crustaceans include crabs, lobsters, and shrimp. Crustaceans are carnivorous, which means that they eat other fish. Because of their diet, crustaceans have moderate levels of cholesterol (60 to 160 mgs. cholesterol per 3½ ounce serving). Of these species, shrimp has the highest cholesterol levels, at 125 to 180 mgs. cholesterol per 3½ ounce serving. **But** shrimp is very low in calories, total fat, and saturated fat, and is high in polyunsaturated fats and omega-3 fatty acids. These qualities make shrimp a good protein choice anyway.

Mollusks include shellfish species such as oysters, mussels, clams, scallops and abalone and are also an excellent seafood choice. Mollusks have the lowest cholesterol, ounce for ounce, of any protein source! Mollusks' diet affects their cholesterol levels, just as with crustaceans. Mollusks are filter-feeders and their diet consists of vegetable matter (phytoplankton). Mollusks have a cholesterol level ranging from 25 to 50 mgs. cholesterol per 3½ ounce serving. They have substantial amounts of non-cholesterol sterols which interfere with the absorption of cholesterol in the body. Lastly, mollusks are rich sources of iron, copper and zinc.

Squid is noteworthy because it actually has the highest cholesterol of any seafood–about 230 mgs. per 3½ ounce serving. As with other shellfish, though, it is very low in fat with less than one percent of its calories coming from fat. Squid does not significantly change blood triglyceride or cholesterol levels and can be included in a heart-healthy diet in moderation.

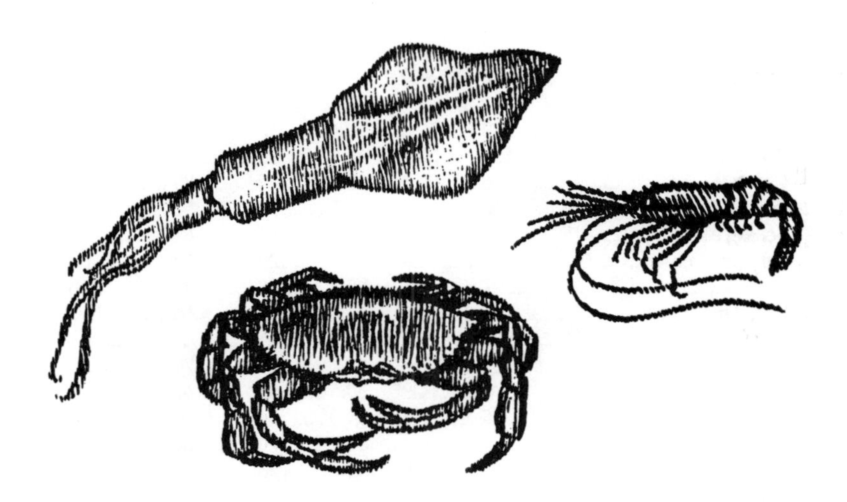

NUTRITIONAL BREAKDOWN OF FISH

100 grams, $3^1/_2$ oz. Raw, edible portion	*HF MF LF	Calories	Protein (grams)	Fat (grams)	Sodium (mgs)	Cholesterol (mgs)	Omega-3 fatty acids (grams)
Bass, freshwater	MF	114	18.9	3.6	70	68	0.3
Bluefish	MF	124	20.0	4.2	60	59	1.2
Catfish, Channel	MF	116	18.2	4.3	63	58	0.3
Cod, Atlantic	LF	82	17.8	0.7	54	43	0.3
Cod, Pacific	LF	82	17.9	0.6	70	40	0.2
Croaker	LF	85	18.0	0.8	80	50	0.2
Flounder	LF	90	18.1	1.4	56	50	0.2
Grouper	LF	87	19.3	0.5	80	50	0.3
Haddock	LF	80	18.2	0.5	60	60	0.2
Halibut	LF	105	20.9	1.2	60	50	0.4
Herring	HF	150	18.3	8.5	75	80	1.7
Hoki	LF	74	15.7	0.8	109	30	0.3
Lingcod	LF	85	17.6	1.1	59	52	0.2
Mackerel	HF	160	21.9	7.3	80	40	2.5
Mahi Mahi	LF	102	21.0	1.0	130	85	0.1
Monkfish	LF	70	15.5	1.0	18	35	N/A
Orange Roughy	LF	65	14.7	0.3	63	58	0.1
Perch, Ocean	LF	95	19.0	1.5	70	60	0.2
Pollock	LF	85	19.5	0.8	60	50	0.5
Pompano	HF	164	18.5	9.8	65	50	0.6
Rockfish (snapper)	LF	97	18.9	1.8	50	40	0.5
Sablefish (black cod)	HF	130	17.9	5.7	55	65	1.5
Salmon:							
Chinook	HF	180	20.0	10.4	45	66	1.4
Chum	MF	120	20.0	3.8	50	74	0.6
Coho	MF	146	21.6	5.6	46	39	0.8
Pink	MF	116	19.9	3.5	67	52	1.0
Sockeye	MF	168	21.3	8.6	47	62	1.2
Salmon, canned	MF	160	21.8	8.0	420	62	1.2
Sea Bass	LF	97	18.4	2.0	68	41	0.6
Shark, Thresher	LF	90	20.0	1.0	50	N/A	N/A
Skate	LF	95	20.0	1.0	N/A	N/A	N/A
Smelt	MF	97	17.6	2.4	60	70	0.7
Sole	LF	70	14.9	0.5	55	45	0.1
Sturgeon	MF	105	16.1	4.0	284	N/A	0.3
Swordfish	MF	120	19.4	4.4	70	50	0.2
Tilefish	LF	90	18.6	1.2	53	N/A	0.4
Tuna, Albacore	MF	102	18.2	3.0	50	25	1.3
Tuna, water-packed	LF	130	29.6	0.5	356	20	0.1
Trout, Rainbow	HF	195	21.5	11.4	52	50	0.5
Whiting	LF	95	21.3	1.2	50	20	0.4

Nutritional Breakdown of Shellfish

100 grams, 3½ oz. Raw, edible portion	*HF MF LF	Calories	Protein (grams)	Fat (grams)	Sodium (mgs)	Cholesterol (mgs)	Omega-3 fatty acids (grams)
CRUSTACEANS							
Crab, Alaskan	LF	75	15.2	0.8	70	60	0.3
Crab, Blue	LF	87	18.0	1.1	293	78	0.3
Crab, Dungeness	LF	81	17.3	1.3	266	59	0.3
Crab, imitation	LF	90	13.4	0.1	600	50	0.2
Lobster	LF	90	16.9	1.7	210	85	0.2
Shrimp	LF	90	18.8	0.8	140	158	0.3
MOLLUSKS							
Abalone	LF	105	17.1	0.8	301	85	trace
Clams	LF	80	11.0	1.5	80	40	0.1
Mussels	LF	75	12.2	1.6	80	25	0.5
Octopus	LF	76	15.0	1.5	N/A	122	0.2
Oysters	LF	81	9.5	2.3	106	50	0.7
Scallops	LF	82	15.3	0.2	160	50	0.2
Squid	LF	85	16.4	0.9	160	230	0.4
FISH OILS (Per Tablespoon)							
Cod liver oil		129	0	14.3	0	81	2.6
Herring oil		129	0	14.3	0	109	1.6
MenHaden oil		129	0	14.3	0	74	2.9
MaxEPA Concentrated fish body oil		129	0	14.3	0	86	4.2
Salmon oil		129	0	14.3	0	69	2.8

NOTE: Use these figures only as a guide. Values vary with species, water temperature, catch location, season caught, etc.

***HF–High Fat Fish:** over 5% fat content

MF–Medium Fat Fish: 2.5%-5% fat content

LF–Low Fat Fish: under 2.5% fat content

N/A–Not Available

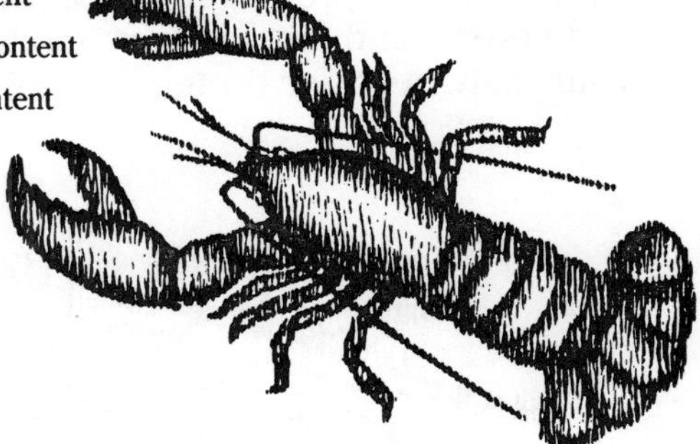

GUIDELINES FOR HEALTHY LIVING

Along with including more seafood in your diet, it is important to enjoy an overall healthier diet. The Surgeon General, the National Research Council, The American Heart Association and the National Cancer Institute all recommend the same basic nutritional guidelines to prevent heart disease and to reduce the risk of other major chronic diseases for which diet is a risk factor.

GUIDELINES INCLUDE:

- **Eat a Well-Balanced Diet.**
- **Reduce Total Fat and Cholesterol.**
- **Increase Complex Carbohydrates, Insoluble and Soluble Fibers.**
- **Limit Protein Consumption.**
- **Limit Salt Consumption.**
- **Limit Calories to Achieve and Maintain a Desirable Weight.**
- **Start and Maintain an Exercise Program.**
- **Minimize Your Consumption of Alcohol.**
- **Seek Professional Advice.**

■ **Eat a well-balanced diet.** Introduce a variety of foods into your diet: lean protein sources, fruits, vegetables, whole grains and cereals and low fat dairy foods. Variety will help you meet your daily need for protein, vitamins and minerals.

■ **Reduce total fat and limit cholesterol.** Reduce total fat–both saturated and unsaturated–to less than 30% of your total calories. Total fat should be divided between the three types of fats: less than 10% polyunsaturated fats, 10-15% monounsaturated fats and no more than 10% saturated fats. Limit cholesterol intake to no more than 300 mgs. per day.

Reduce saturated fats in your diet. It is important to decrease both the total fat and the saturated fat in the diet. Saturated fats may contribute more to high blood cholesterol and LDL levels than any other type of fat. Saturated fats are found mainly in animal products such as meat, butter, cheese and lard, and are usually solid at room temperature. Tropical oils such as coconut, cocoa butter, palm and palm kernel are highly saturated fats. Hydrogenated vegetable oils such as Crisco shortening are also saturated fats.

Increase unsaturated fats in your diet. Both polyunsaturated and monounsaturated fats help lower serum cholesterol levels. There are two major families of polyunsaturated fats: omega-6 fatty acids from vegetables and omega-3 fatty acids from fish oils. Vegetable oils high in omega-6's are corn, cottonseed, safflower, sunflower, sesame and soybean oils. Omega-3's are found predominantly in seafood. Monounsaturated fats are typically found in olives, olive oil, canola oil, peanut oil and avocados. Recent research has shown that when polyunsaturated and monounsaturated fats replace saturated fats in the diet, beneficial changes occur in blood cholesterol levels.

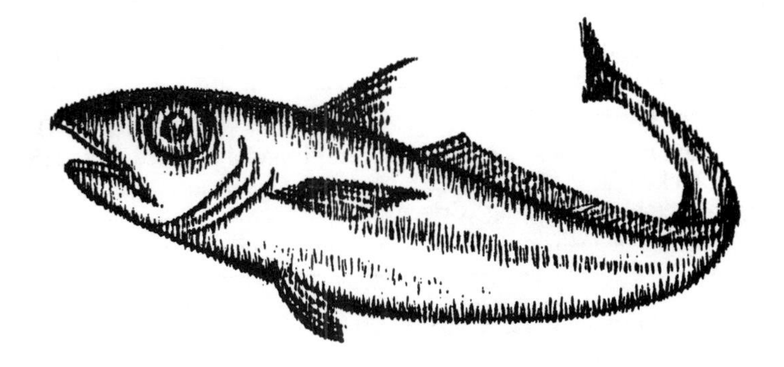

Monitor dietary fats and blood cholesterol. Blood cholesterol level is a risk factor for coronary heart disease. But, it is the type and amount of fat that we eat that may be just as important in determining blood cholesterol levels as the amount of cholesterol we eat. The goal of a heart-healthy diet is to reduce low density lipoproteins (LDL's) while maintaining or increasing the level of high density lipoproteins (HDL's), as well as lowering cholesterol levels.

LDL's carry cholesterol to the body tissues. Higher levels of LDL's are associated with heart disease. HDL's carry cholesterol away from body tissues and help prevent heart disease. An easy way to remember the difference between LDL's and HDL's is to think of LDL's as "Less Desirable Lipids" and HDL's as "Highly Desirable Lipids."

All Oils Are Not Created Equal

Any fat that is solid at room temperature is more likely to raise blood cholesterol levels than one that is liquid–no matter whether it comes from animal (lard) or vegetable (margarine). The less saturated the fat the better. Health professionals often recommend tub or liquid margarines and polyunsaturated oils.

LIQUID OILS	% SATURATED FAT
Canola	7%
Safflower	9%
Sunflower	10%
Corn	13%
Olive	13%
Soybean	14%
Peanut	17%
Liquid and soft tub margarines (average of several brands)	18%
Cottonseed	26%

SOLID FATS	% SATURATED FAT
Stick margarines (average of several brands)	19%
Chicken fat	30%
Vegetable shortening (Crisco)	31%
Lard	40%
Palm oil	49%
Butter	62%
Palm kernel oil	81%
Coconut oil	86%

Tips on Selecting a Polyunsaturated Margarine

Look for the following information on labels for best margarine choices:

■ The type of fat in a margarine can be polyunsaturated (acceptable), monounsaturated (acceptable) or saturated (unacceptable).

■ If nutrition labeling is included, the greater the amount of polyunsaturated or monounsaturated fat compared to saturated fat the better.

■ The ingredient list should have a "liquid" vegetable oil listed first, followed by hydrogenated or partially hydrogenated vegetable oil.

■ Safflower oil is highest in polyunsaturated fat, followed by sunflower, corn, soybean, cottonseed and sesame oils. Any of these oils are acceptable.

■ Look for new margarines containing canola oil, a monounsaturated oil which is acceptable.

■ Avoid margarines which contain coconut or palm kernel oil, because these are highly saturated fats.

■ Soft margarines (tub or liquid) are usually higher in polyunsaturated fat than stick margarines.

An example of an acceptable margarine label would read as follows:

Ingredients: Liquid sunflower oil, partially hydrogenated soybean oil, sweet dairy whey, water, partially hydrogenated cottonseed oil, salt, vegetable mono and diglycerides, soy lecithin, potassium sorbate and citric acids added as preservatives, artificially flavored, colored with beta carotene, vitamins A and D added.

Nutrition Information Per Serving

Serving size	14 grams (1 tablespoon)
Servings per pound	32
Calories	90
Protein	0 grams
Carbohydrate	0 grams
Fat	10 grams
Percent of calories from fat	99%
Polyunsaturated	4 grams
Saturated	2 grams
Cholesterol	0 mgs.
Sodium	90 mgs.

■ **Increase complex carbohydrates, insoluble and soluble fibers.** Increase your consumption of foods that contain complex carbohydrates, such as whole grain breads and cereal products, vegetables (especially dried beans and peas) and fruits. A high fiber diet may help prevent some types of cancer as well as preventing constipation. For people trying to lose weight, a high fiber meal provides a greater sense of satisfaction after eating.

- Daily, enjoy at least one serving of citrus fruit such as oranges or grapefruit.
- Eat more cabbage-family vegetables such as broccoli, cauliflower, cabbage, brussels sprouts and kale.
- Choose more foods with vitamin A such as carrots, peaches, apricots, squash and broccoli.
- Eat more soluble fiber. Soluble fibers may help reduce blood cholesterol and triglyceride levels. Include 3 to 4 servings per day of foods high in soluble fiber, such as oatmeal, oat, corn or barley bran, apples, pears and citrus fruits, dried peas, beans and lentils, as well as many other vegetables, to help the body eliminate cholesterol.

■ **Limit protein consumption.** The average intake of protein by Americans greatly exceeds the U.S. Recommended Daily Allowance (RDA). Limit protein consumption to 15% to 20% of total calories per day or eat a maximum of 6 ounces of protein per day.

■ **Limit salt consumption.** Reduce intake of sodium by choosing foods relatively low in sodium. Limit the amount of salt added in food preparation, and at the table, to less than one teaspoon per day.

■ **Limit calories to achieve and maintain a desirable body weight.** The best way to lose weight–and keep it off–is to follow a low calorie and low fat diet. For safe, effective and permanent weight loss, the American Dietetic Association recommends a weight loss of one to two pounds per week.

■ **Start and maintain an exercise program.** Regular exercise improves your chances of sticking to a weight-loss program and will help keep the weight off over the long-term. Choose a form of exercise that you enjoy.

Aerobic exercise–the kind that keeps your body moving and increases your pulse and breathing rates–is good for your heart and lungs. It also is a great way to burn calories. Walking briskly, running, biking and swimming are all excellent choices.

■ **Minimize your consumption of alcohol.** Use alcohol in moderation and avoid drinking when pregnant.

■ **Seek professional advice.** Ask your doctor or registered dietitian for specific advice before making major dietary or lifestyle changes.

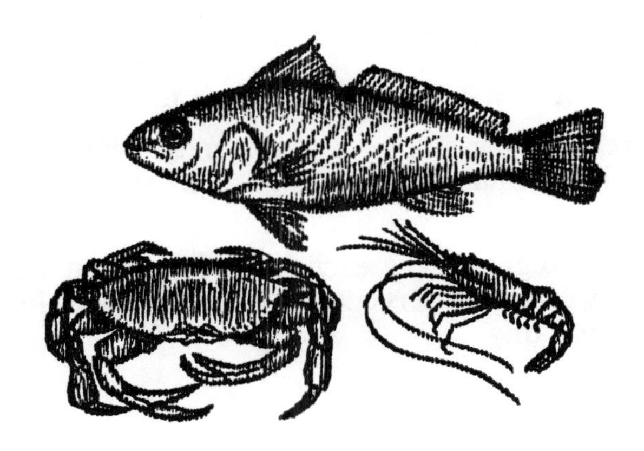

WEIGHT LOSS GUIDE

One of the greatest challenges faced by dieters is to stick to a weight-loss, then weight-maintenance, program throughout a lifetime. Aiming for a lifetime program is critical when starting a healthier and lighter meal plan. Once you have made up your mind to change eating patterns, set your sights on changing them permanently.

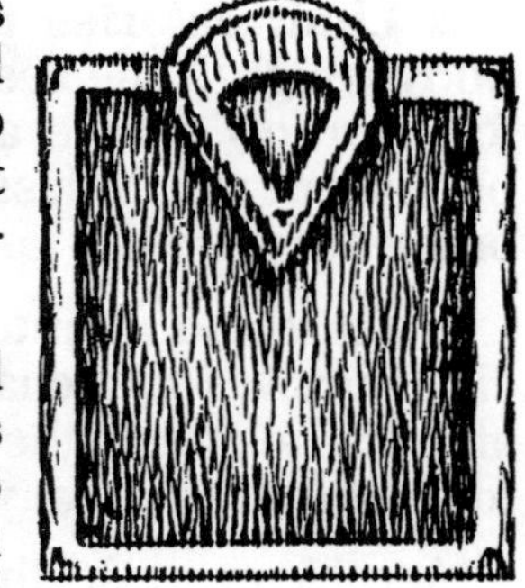

Weight loss should always be gradual at a rate of no more than one to two pounds per week. A consistent weight loss of two pounds per week is a good indication you are losing excess body fat and not vital lean body mass. The American Dietetic Association recommends the following calorie intake guidelines to achieve weight loss of one to two pounds per week:

> *One pound of body fat contains 3500 calories. To lose one to two pounds of weight per week you need to eat 500 to 1,000 calories less a day than you usually eat for 7 days. The minimum recommended calorie level per day is 1200 calories for women and 1500 calories for men. Ensure the diet includes all necessary vitamins and minerals.*

Here are a few helpful weight-loss tips:

- Exercise at least three to five times per week. Regular exercise is important for weight loss and weight maintenance.
- Eat three regular meals each day and do not eat "on the run." Making each meal an occasion will help you avoid between-meal snacking.

- For those times when between-meal cravings do occur, keep a supply of pre-cut raw vegetables such as carrots, celery or broccoli on hand in an airtight container. If time is short, keep small-sized vegetables available. Cherry tomatoes, radishes, baby carrots and sugar snap peas don't even require cutting.
- Watch portion sizes. Limiting portion sizes is an effective way to cut back on calories.
- Put thought and creativity into the way you prepare and serve your food. Elegant spas serve their clients modest portions of low calorie foods arranged as a feast for the eyes. Add crunch and color to make meals appetizing and appealing.
- Cook foods with little or no added fat. Good methods are baking, broiling, poaching, sautéing, and steaming.
- Limit intake of high fat foods and snack items such as butter, margarine, oils, desserts, salad dressings, mayonnaise, chips and cookies.
- For a snack in front of the television, enjoy a bowl of hot-air popped popcorn. It's low in calories and high in fiber. While microwave popcorn varieties are convenient, many can be high in fat content. Check the label for fat content.
- Substitute low fat products for higher fat products such as skim milk for whole milk and part-skim mozzarella cheese for cheddar cheese. (See page 32.)

LIGHTEN UP WITH SEAFOOD

- Stock up on frozen, unbreaded fish and shellfish. Each time you go to the seafood store or supermarket, check for items on sale. You'll never be short of this low calorie diet staple. Today's "frozen-at-sea" technology means that premium-quality frozen fish is always available.
- Select water-packed tuna over oil-packed varieties as it is significantly lower in calories. A 3½ ounce can of light tuna packed in oil, then drained, still contains 200 calories; the same tuna packed in water and drained has only 130 calories.
- Surimi products are an inexpensive addition to a diet plan. Surimi (for example, imitation crabmeat) is made from white fish such as pollock and is very low in calories (only 90 calories per 3½ ounce serving). Include it in a green salad for lunch.
- Serve a seafood appetizer or soup before dinner to cut your appetite. Try boiled shrimp spritzed with fresh lemon juice, or smoked salmon with a tray of fresh-cut vegetables. Pickled herring or pickled salmon are also good light choices to start the evening meal.
- Save time by poaching two fish or shellfish meals at once, serve one immediately and save the second for lunch the next day.

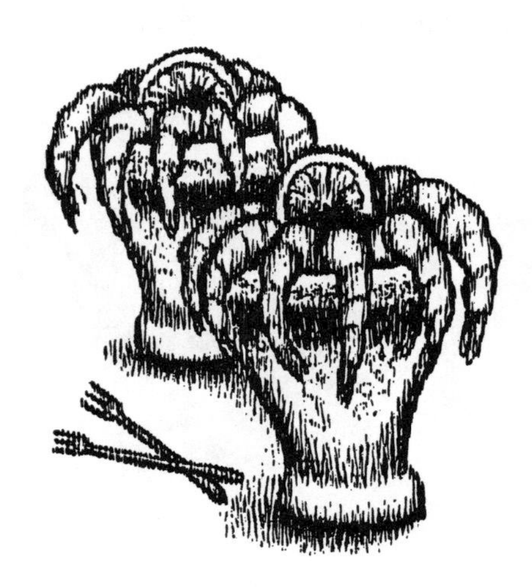

- Start an entertaining tradition with Italian Cioppino (see page 93) – a dish that family and friends will love. Have guests bring their favorite seafood prepared in bite-sized pieces to add to the cioppino. Before serving, add all seafood to cioppino base and cook until done for a seafood extravaganza. Serve with French bread and green salad. Always a hit!
- Seafood barbecues are a dieter's dream. Start a picnic with grilled salmon or shark kabobs brushed with teriyaki sauce. Round out the meal with shrimp, coleslaw, corn on the cob and watermelon slices.
- Selecting last-minute dinner ingredients from the supermarket salad bar is becoming commonplace. You can create a prep-free stir-fry by buying shrimp, scallops, halibut or other fish from the seafood counter, then picking up some mushrooms, celery, carrots and broccoli from the salad bar.
- Flying? Stay away from calorie laden airplane meals. Order special meals in advance. Seafood meals, often including cold shrimp plate or seafood salads, are generally available.

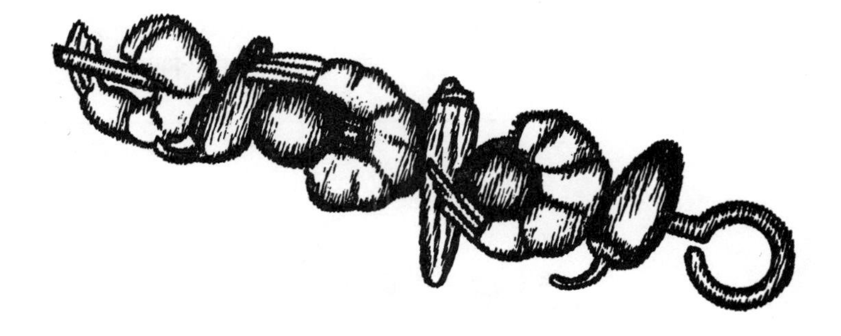

LIGHTEN UP YOUR RECIPES

Preparing a low-calorie, heart-healthy meal can be easy. The following list gives examples of substitutions to make your recipes lighter and healthier. These substitutions are used in developing all recipes.

Original Ingredient	Lighter Substitutions
Cream cheese	Blended or processed low fat cottage cheese, non-fat quark
Mayonnaise	Blended or processed low fat cottage cheese, plain low fat yogurt, reduced-calorie mayonnaise
Sour cream	Plain low fat yogurt, blended or processed low fat cottage cheese with a little lemon juice added
Heavy cream	Evaporated whole, or preferably, evaporated skim milk
Whole milk cottage cheese	Low fat cottage cheese
Butter, lard	Non-stick vegetable spray Polyunsaturated oils and margarines made with corn, cottonseed, safflower, sesame seed, soybean or sunflower oils Monounsaturated oils such as olive oil, peanut oil or canola oil
Cheddar cheese	Part-skim mozzarella cheese or ricotta cheese, Farmer's cheese, non-fat quark

Original Ingredient	Lighter Substitutions
Whole egg	Two egg whites or 1/4 cup egg substitute
Soy sauce	Low sodium soy sauce
Chicken broth	Low sodium chicken broth
Salt, onion salt, garlic salt	Herbs and spices can be combined in creative ways to make recipes more flavorful. Instead of using your salt shaker, try cooking with these herbs and spices to enhance flavor:
	allspice, basil, bay leaf, cayenne pepper, celery seed, celery leaves, chervil, curry powder, dill seed, dill weed, fennel seed, garlic powder, marjoram, mustard, nutmeg, onion powder, oregano, paprika, parsley, rosemary, saffron, tarragon, thyme
Condiments	lemons, limes, wine, vermouth, sherry, Dijon mustard, Worcestershire sauce, horseradish

1/4 teaspoon powdered herbs = 1/4 to 1/2 teaspoon crumbled herbs = 2 teaspoons fresh herbs

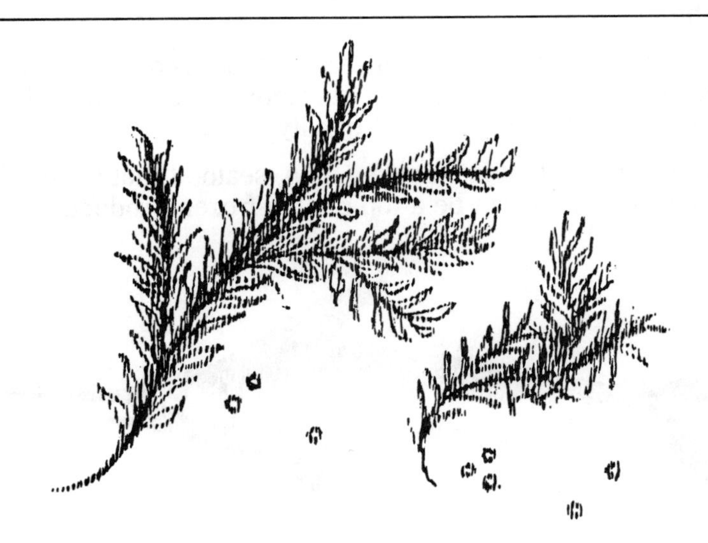

HOW TO SHOP FOR SEAFOOD

TEN TOP TIPS FOR SHOPPING FOR SEAFOOD

Leading seafood retailers around the country agree, if you follow these ten steps to purchasing seafood at the seafood counter you will be assured of an excellent quality product.

1. Ask friends and acquaintances for recommendations of the best seafood counters in your area.
2. Establish a relationship with your seafood salesperson. He is apt to feel more responsible for your success with seafood buying and preparation.
3. Ask the seafood salesperson what he would recommend for dinner. He is often likely to suggest the freshest and best quality seafood on hand.
4. Use your senses in making a seafood purchase. Smell product or package. Seafood should not smell unpleasant, but like fresh ocean breezes. Look to make sure seafood, wrapped in packages, is not sitting in excess liquid. Seafood should be free of blood, bruises and discolorations. Press fish with thumb to make sure product is firm and elastic to the touch.
5. Purchase seafood that is in season. Just as corn on the cob is freshest in the summer, seafood species have their individual seasons for best quality.
6. Buy seafood that is on sale. Often, seafood that is on sale is in season or can be a top quality frozen product.

7. Purchase frozen seafood products. As modern processing methods have improved dramatically, frozen fish and shellfish is virtually interchangeable with fresh fish and shellfish in terms of nutritive value, appearance and flavor. If frozen seafood is not on display, request that the seafood salesperson provide you with the frozen product. This is an easy way to stock your freezer and have a supply of seafood on hand.

8. After shopping for your seafood, be sure to return home and put it in the refrigerator as soon as possible. Keeping seafood at proper temperatures is critical to maintaining a fresh product.

9. In warmer climates, or if you will be delayed in returning home, ask your seafood salesperson to wrap your seafood in ice. Have your seafood bagged with other cold or frozen products or carry a small ice chest in the car.

10. If you ever do buy a seafood product that is past its prime, return the product to the seafood counter and voice your complaint to the seafood salesperson or store manager. They need to know! On the other hand, if you enjoy a seafood meal, let them know that, too!

SEAFOOD SUBSTITUTIONS

This profile groups together fish of similar flavor, richness and color. The different seafoods in each category taste somewhat alike and can be prepared the same way. If, for example, a recipe calls for a fish that is unavailable in your area, you can use another from the same group in its place.

FISH

Very light, delicate flavor

- Alaska Pollock
- Brook Trout
- Chilean Sea Bass
- Cod
- Dover Sole
- Giant Sea Bass
- Grouper
- Haddock
- Hoki
- Lake Whitefish
- Orange Roughy
- Pacific Halibut
- Pacific Ocean Perch
- Pacific Sanddab
- Petrale Sole
- Rainbow Trout
- Rex Sole
- Smelt
- Summer Flounder
- Walleye
- White Sea Bass
- Yellowtail Flounder
- Yellowtail Snapper

Light to moderate flavor

- American Plaice/Dab
- Arrowtooth Flounder
- Atlantic Ocean Perch
- Atlantic Salmon
- Black Seabass
- Bluefish
- Buffalofish
- Burbot
- Butterfish
- Carp
- Catfish
- Chum Salmon
- Crevalle Jack
- Croaker
- English Sole
- Greenland Turbot
- Jewfish
- King (Chinook) Salmon
- Lake Chub
- Lake Herring
- Lake Sturgeon
- Lake Trout
- Lingcod
- Mahi Mahi
- Mako Shark
- Monkfish
- Mullet
- Northern Pike
- Pacific Whiting
- Perch
- Pink Salmon
- Pollock
- Pompano
- Red Snapper
- Rock Sole
- Rockfish
- Sablefish
- Sand Shark
- Scup/Porgie
- Sheepshead
- Silver (Coho) Salmon
- Snook
- Sockeye (Red) Salmon
- Spotted Sea Trout
- Starry Flounder
- Striped Bass
- Swordfish
- Tilapia
- Tuna
- White King Salmon
- White Sea Trout
- Whiting
- Winter Flounder
- Wolffish

More pronounced flavor

- Atlantic Mackerel
- King Mackerel
- Spanish Mackerel

SHELLFISH

Crustaceans (Crab, Lobster, Shrimp)

- Alaska King Crab
- Blue Crab
- Dungeness Crab
- Jonah Crab
- Red Crab
- Soft Shell Crab
- Snow Crab
- Stone Crab

- American Lobster
- Rock Lobster
- Slipper Lobster
- Spiny Lobster

- Brown Shrimp
- Cold Water Shrimp Meat
- Northern Shrimp
- Pink Shrimp
- Rock Shrimp
- Red Shrimp
- Tiger Shrimp
- White Shrimp

Mollusks (Clams, Scallops, Oysters, Mussels)

- Butter Clam
- Geoduck Clam
- Hard or Quahog Clam
- Littleneck Clam
- Pismo Clam
- Razor Clam
- Soft Clam/Steamer
- Surf or Skinner Clam

- Bay Scallop
- Sea Scallop
- Calico Scallop

- Eastern/Atlantic Oyster
- Gulf Oyster
- Olympia Oyster
- Pacific Oyster
- South American Oyster

- California Mussel
- Blue Mussel
- Green Shell Mussel

Others

- Octopus
- Squid
- Crawfish

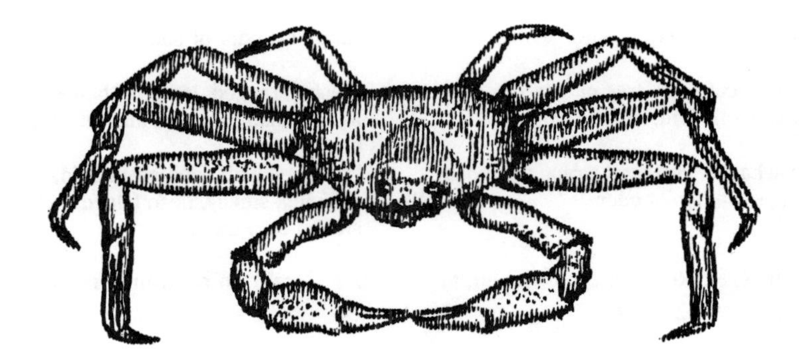

HOW TO SELECT TOP QUALITY SEAFOOD AT THE SEAFOOD COUNTER

FRESH WHOLE FISH

Good Quality	Poor Quality
Clear eyes, bright, bulging; black pupil	Dull eyes, sunken, cloudy; gray pupil
Bright red gills, free of slime; clear mucus	Brown to grayish gills; thick, yellow mucus
Flesh firm and elastic to touch, tight to bone	Flesh soft and flabby, separating from bone
Ocean-fresh odor, slight seaweed scent	Ammonia odor, sour smell
Scales adhere tightly to skin, bright color, very few missing	Dull scales, large quantities missing
Belly cavity (if gutted) clean, washed, blood-free intestinal cavity	Belly cavity (if gutted) has cuts, bones loose from flesh, bloody, poorly cleaned

STORAGE: Refrigerate, covered, at 32°- 40°F. Ice body cavity. Drain off accumulated water daily. Store 1-2 days. Freeze promptly if not going to cook immediately.

FRESH FILLETS/STEAKS

Good Quality	Poor Quality
Color varies with species, but should be consistent throughout meat, bright	Color shows bruising, red spots, yellowing or browning at edges
Ocean-fresh odor, slight seaweed scent	Ammonia odor or sour smell
Clean-cut flesh, free of skin (if skinless), firm, moist	Flesh is ragged, traces of bones and skin (if skinless), soft and mushy, dried out
Packaged with tight wrapping, moist-appearing, mild odor	Packaged with excessive liquid, dripping, smelly, flesh folded and stuffed onto tray

STORAGE: Refrigerate, covered, at 32°- 40°F. Drain off accumulated water daily. Store 1-2 days.

CANNED SEAFOOD

Good Quality	Poor Quality
■ Cans full, not dented, free from foreign matter, vacuum sealed	■ Cans leaking, bulging, no vacuum seal

STORAGE: Dry area. Store 6-9 months.

FROZEN FISH AND SHELLFISH

Good Quality	Poor Quality
■ Flesh is solidly frozen, glossy. When thawed should pass same criteria as for fresh fish or shellfish	■ Flesh is partially thawed, white or dark spots, signs of drying such as papery edges, discoloration
■ Tight, moisture-proof wrapping, complete packaging	■ Packaging is punctured, shows build-up of ice crystals
■ Should be stacked below load line of freezer case. Temperature 0°	■ Improper storage; excessive glazing

STORAGE: Tightly wrapped, in freezer at 0° to -20°F. Lean fish: Store 4-6 months. Fattier fish: Store 2-3 months.

LIVE SHELLFISH

Crabs, Lobsters, Crustaceans

Good Quality	Poor Quality
■ Legs move when tickled, live lobster tail curls under, heavy weight, hard shell	■ No movement, lobster tail hangs limp, light weight, soft shell (except for blue soft-shelled crab)

STORAGE: Keep alive in well-ventilated refrigerator in leak-proof container. Store covered with damp paper towel. Never store in airtight container as they will suffocate. Store 2-3 days.

MOLLUSKS IN SHELL

Oysters, Mussels, Clams

Good Quality	Poor Quality
■ Shells tightly closed or close when tapped, clean mussels, bearded ■ The neck of a soft-shelled clam should twitch when touched	■ Gaping shells that do not close when tapped; strong, fishy odor

STORAGE: Same as crabs, lobsters, etc.

SHUCKED MOLLUSKS

Good Quality	Poor Quality
■ Body is plump, clear liquor, free of shell particles; liquid less than 15% of volume ■ Jar oysters have pull date	■ Body has a sour odor, shell particles, signs of drying, opaque liquor, excessive liquid (more than 15%)

STORAGE: Store completely covered in leak-proof container. Oysters: Store 1-3 days. Mussels & clams: Store 1-2 days.

SCALLOPS

Good Quality	Poor Quality
■ Body has a creamy white to pinkish color	■ Body has a sour odor; off-color

STORAGE: Refrigerate in leak-proof, covered container with own liquid. Store 1-2 days.

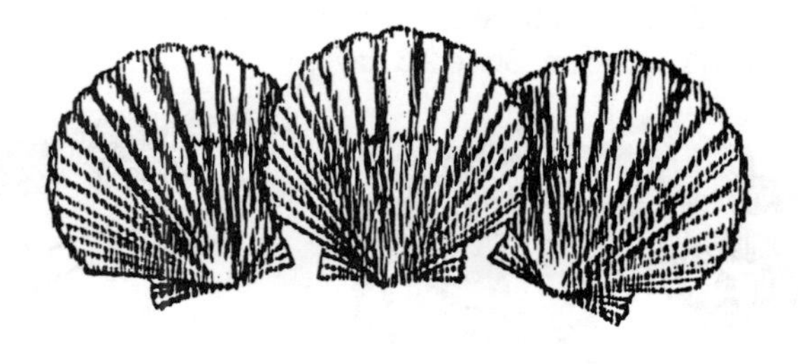

SHRIMP

Good Quality	Poor Quality
■ Body has firm texture, mild odor, cleaned	■ Body has ammonia odor; black spots, soft flesh

STORAGE: Refrigerate in leak-proof container. Drain liquid. Store 1-2 days.

COOKED LOBSTER, CRAB, OR SHRIMP

Good Quality	Poor Quality
■ Body has mild, natural odor	■ Sour odor
■ Flesh has snowy white meat with red or brown tints (depending on species) for crab meat, bright red shell	■ Flesh is slimy to the touch
■ Kept moist, but not in direct contact with ice	

STORAGE: Refrigerate in leak-proof container. Store 1-2 days. Pasteurized crab meat may be stored up to 6 months at 32°F, but once container is opened the crab should be used within 1-2 days.

SURIMI

Good Quality	Poor Quality
■ Ingredients listed	■ Flesh is slimy, dull colored and has a sour odor
■ Very little water in package or tray	■ Too much water in package or tray

STORAGE: Refrigerate covered. Store up to one week.

HOW TO PREPARE SEAFOOD FOR COOKING

Both fresh and frozen fish are marketed in quite a few different forms and it is advantageous to know them. Pick the form suggested in your recipe or the one that seems best suited to the style of preparation.

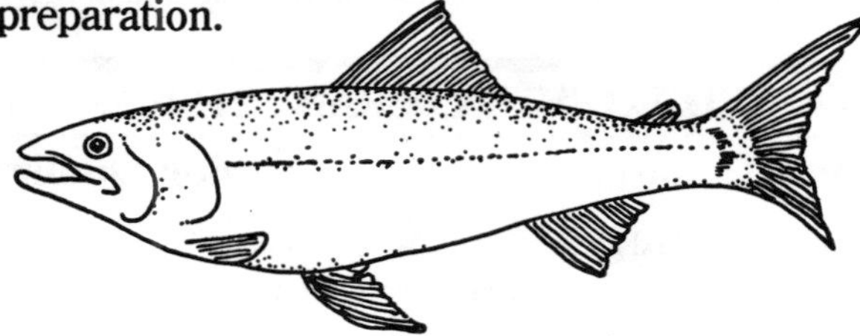

WHOLE OR IN THE ROUND
This, as the terms suggest, means the fish is whole just as it comes from the water. Nothing has been removed. Edible portion: 50%.

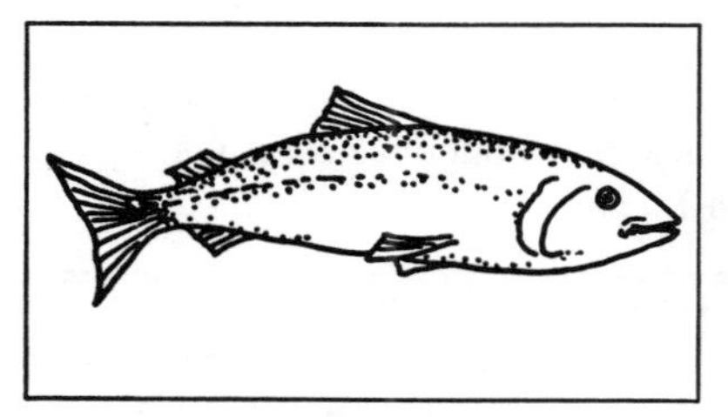

DRAWN
The fish has been gutted. The fins and scales have usually been removed. Edible portion: 50%.

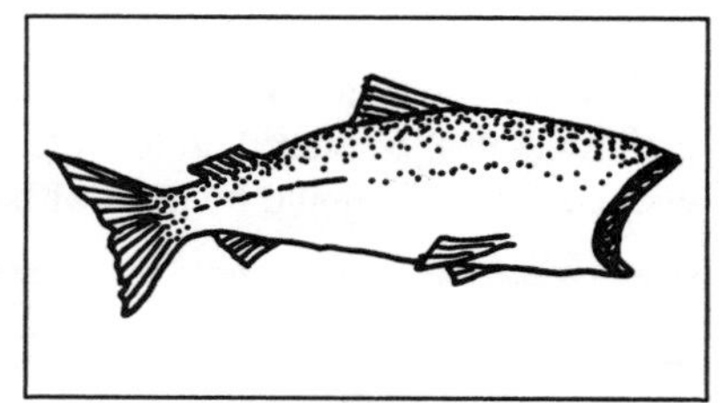

DRESSED
The fish has been gutted and scaled, the fins removed and usually the head and tail cut off. Edible portion: 66%.

FILLETS
Fillets are the sides of the fish cut away from the backbone. They're often boneless and skinless, though the skin of fatty fish is usually left attached to the fillets. (That way it holds together better during cooking.) Sometimes small bones called pins are present. They can be easily removed. Edible portion: 100%.

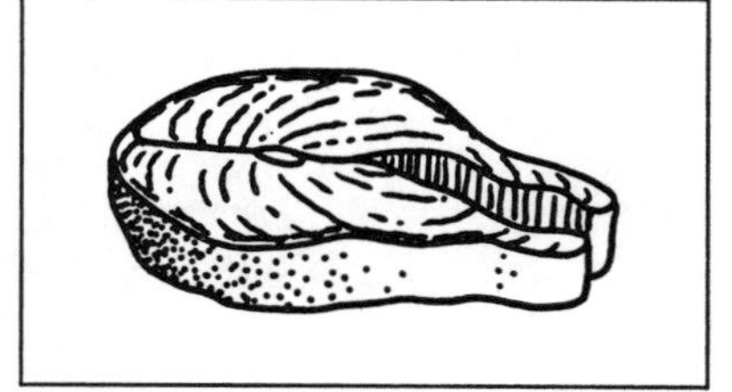

STEAKS
These are the cross-section slices, from ¾ to 1½ inches thick, of larger dressed fish. Steaks usually have a piece of the backbone in the center. Edible portion: 85%.

HOW TO FILLET A ROUND-BODIED FISH

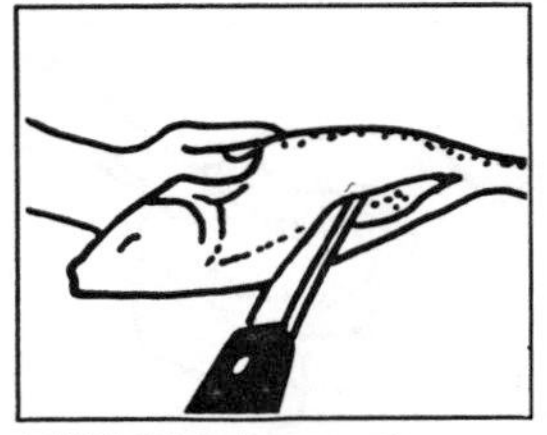

1. With fish facing away from you, use a sharp, thin-bladed knife to cut along the back of the fish, from tail to head. Make a second cut just behind the gills, down to the backbone.

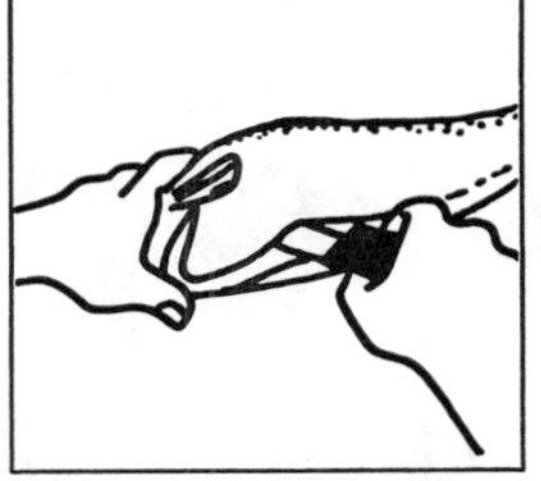

2. Holding the knife at a slight angle, cut along the bone to free the back side of the fillet.

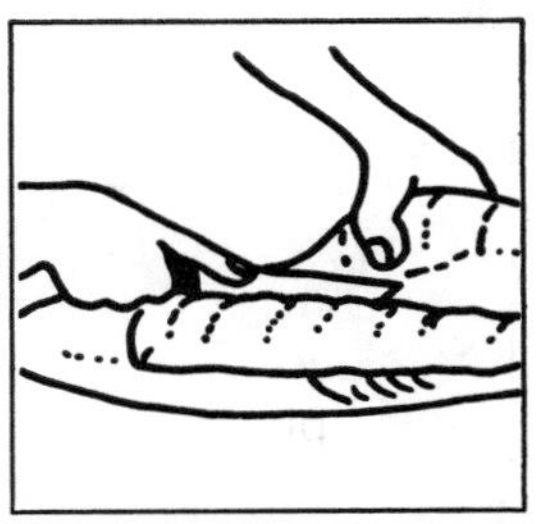

3. Peel back the free meat, then cut fillet away from rib cage. Turn fish over and repeat above steps for second fillet.

HOW TO STEAK A SALMON

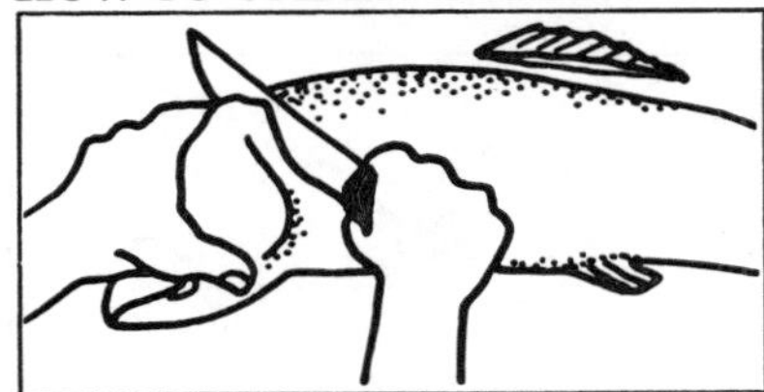

1. Remove fins from cleaned, scaled fish by running knife point along each side of fin base, then pulling fins free. To remove head, make diagonal cut behind the gills and sever backbone with heavy knife or cleaver.

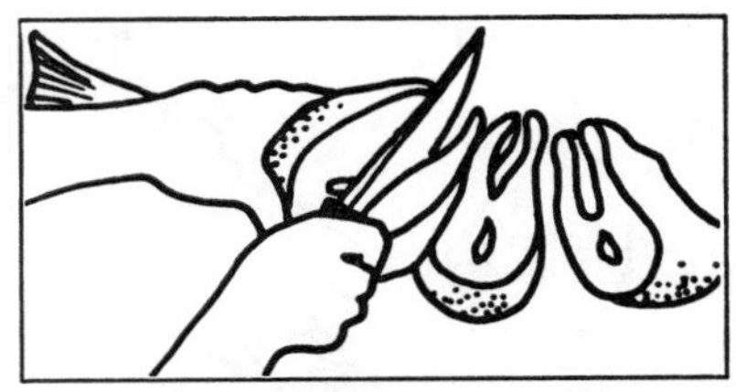

2. Still using a heavy knife, slice fish into steaks about 1 inch thick, starting about 4 inches from the head end. (Reserve unsteaked head-and-tail portions for another use.)

HOW TO FILLET A FLAT FISH

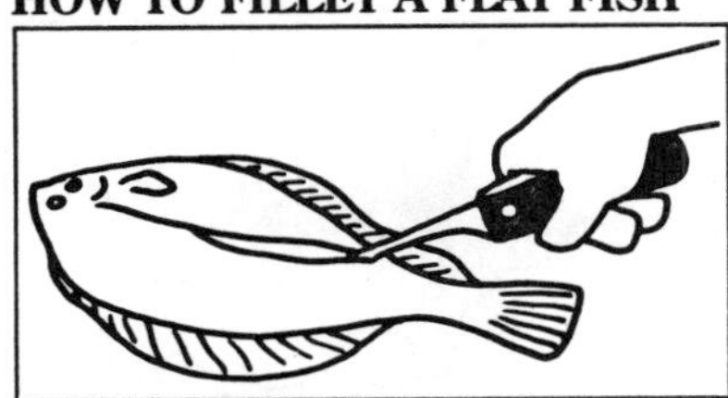

1. With the eyed (dark) side of the flatfish up, use a flexible boning knife to make a cut along the spine from the gills to the tail.

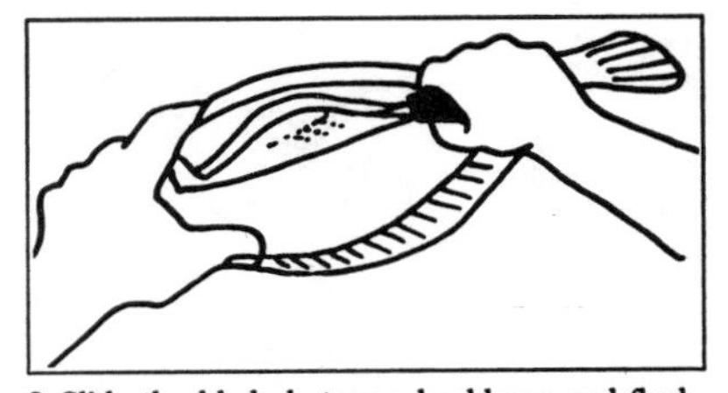

2. Slide the blade between backbone and flesh, lifting the fillet away from the bone. Remove the second fillet in the same manner.

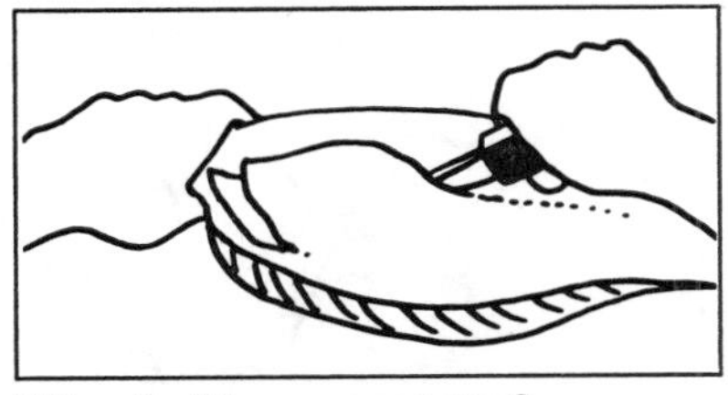

3. Turn the fish over; repeat step 2.

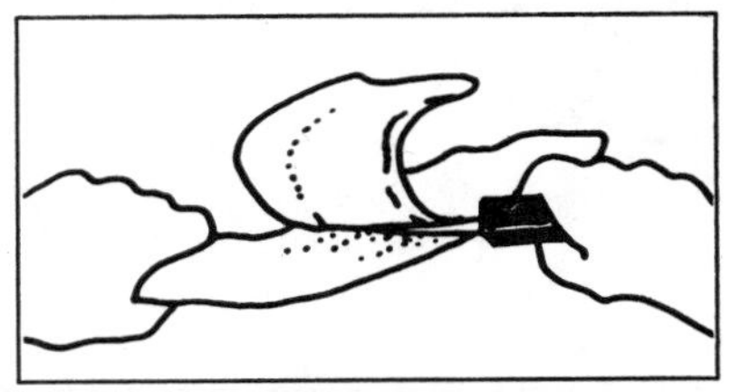

4. To skin, grasp fillet by the tail end, skin side down. Holding the knife at a slight angle, cut the meat free.

HOW TO OPEN A CLAM

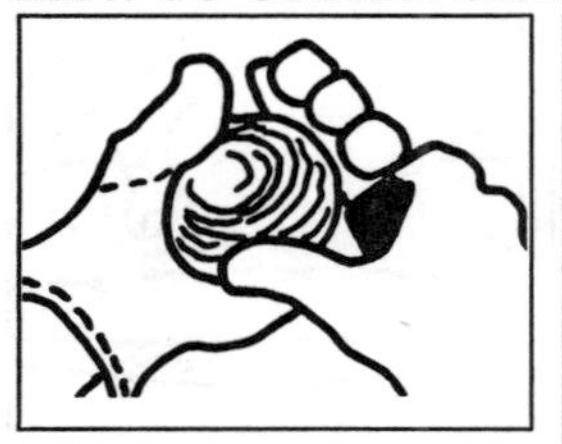

1. Wash clams thoroughly, discarding any that have broken shells or that do not close. Wearing a heavy glove for safety, hold the clam in your palm and force the blade of a clam knife between the shells.

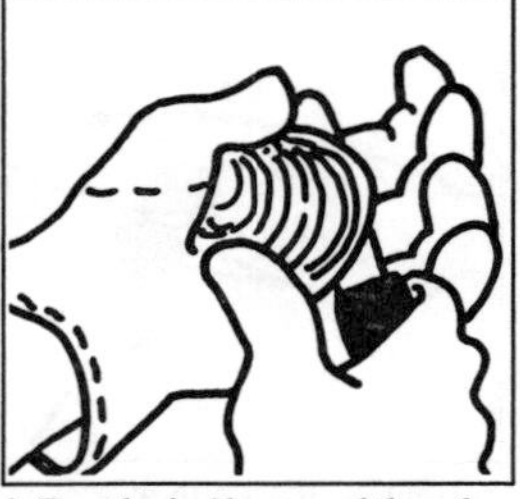

2. Run the knife around the edge of the shell to cut through the muscles holding it together.

3. Open clam and remove top shell. Use knife to loosen clam from bottom shell. Check for shell fragments before serving.

HOW TO SHUCK AN OYSTER

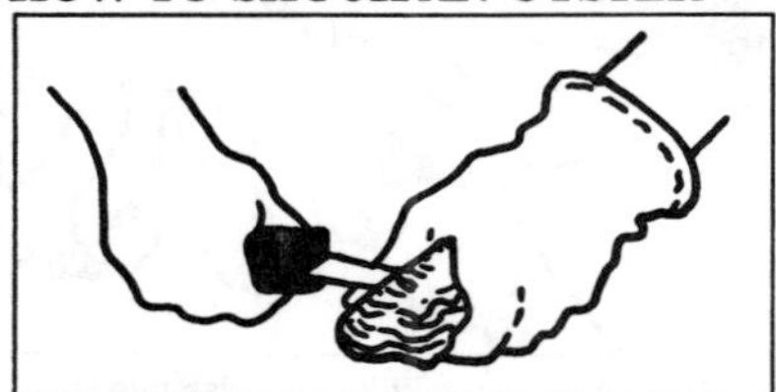

1. Hold oysters under cold running water and scrub with a stiff brush; discard those that are not tightly closed or that do not close quickly when handled. Place oyster, cupped side down, on a firm surface, holding it (with a gloved hand) near the hinge.

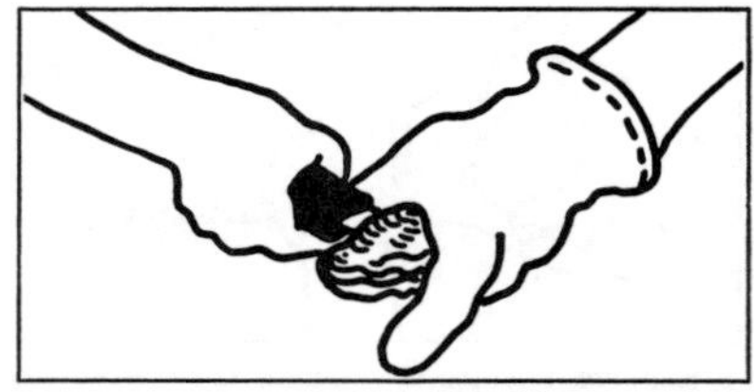

2. Insert an oyster knife in the side opposite the hinge, and twist knife blade to force oyster open.

3. Run the knife around the edge of the shell to cut the muscle that holds the two shells together.

4. Remove top shell, and loosen oyster from bottom shell. Check for shell fragments before serving.

HOW TO CLEAN A MUSSEL

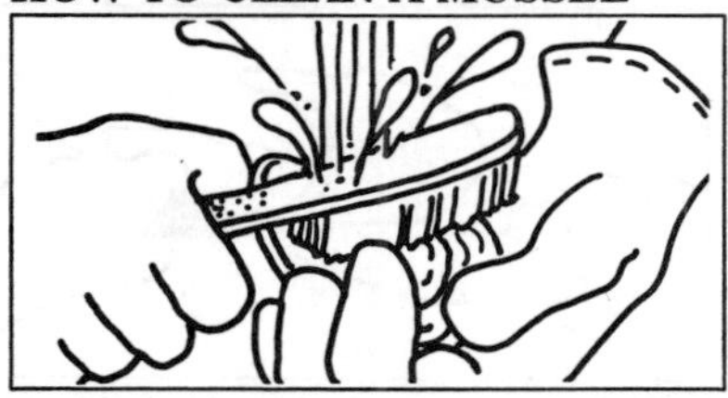

1. Prepare mussels as soon as possible after gathering. To prepare, scrub shells in cold water.

2. Discard any mussels that have open shells or shells that do not close quickly with handling. Clip or pull beard.

HOW TO DRESS A SOFT-SHELL CRAB

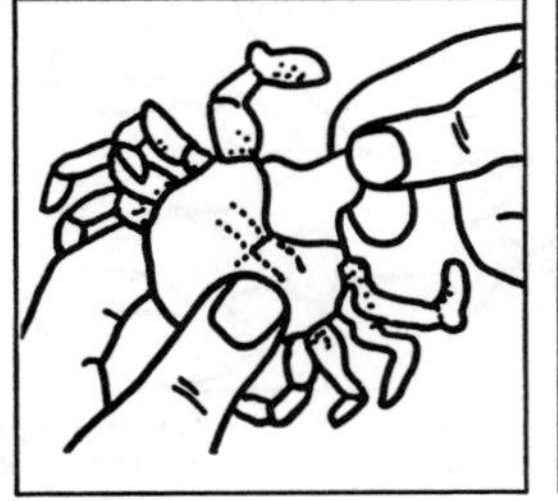

1. Remove the apron, the segmented abdominal part beneath the carapace, or shell.

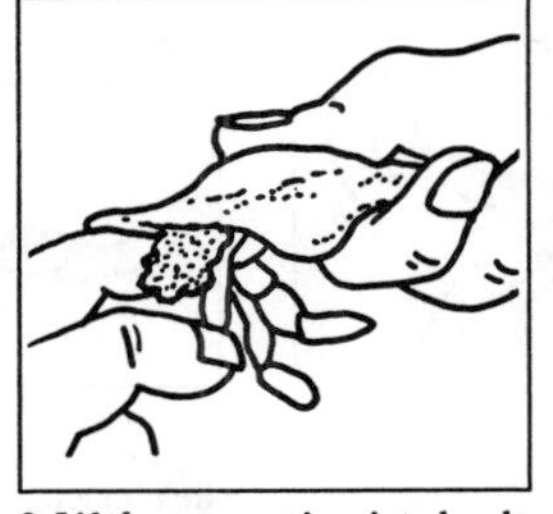

2. Lift the carapace's pointed ends and remove spongy material.

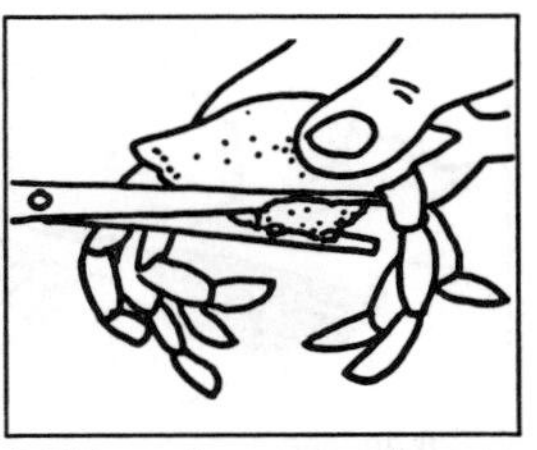

3. Using scissors, cut about 1/2 inch behind the eyes and remove the face of the crab. What remains is the edible portion.

HOW TO CRACK A CRAB

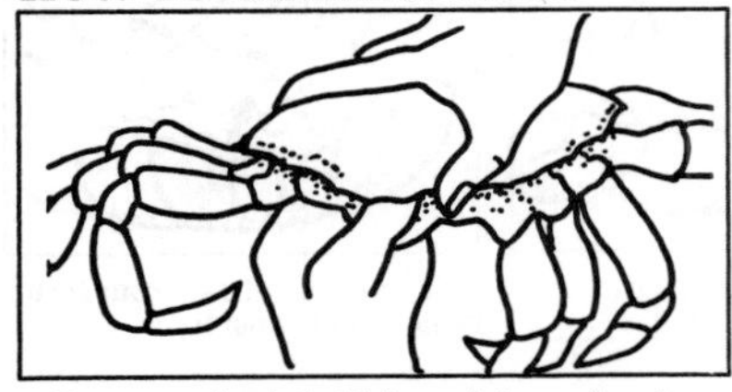

1. To remove back, hold the crab in one hand, pry off the shell with the other.

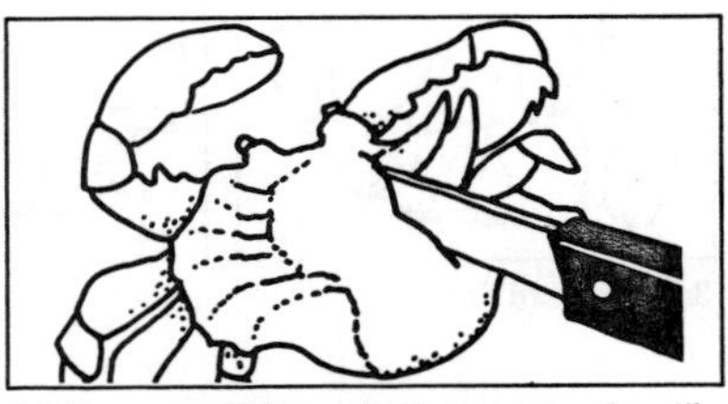

2. Using a small, heavy knife, cut away the gills. Wash out the intestines and spongy matter.

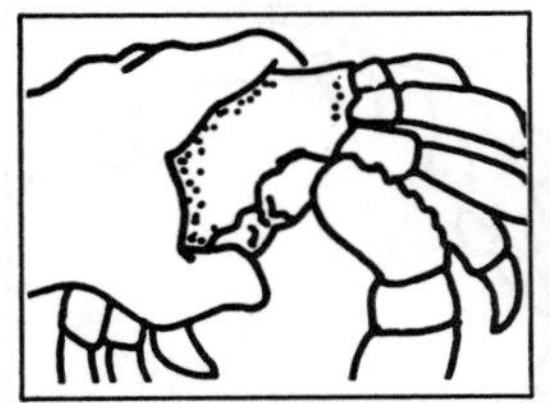

3. Twist legs off. Remove claws and crack. Use knife to pry meat out.

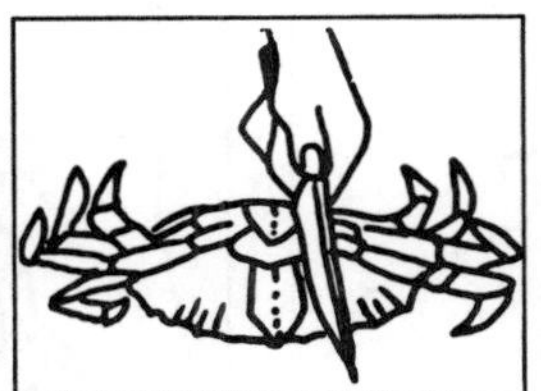

4. Cut the body down the middle, then cut halves into several parts. Remove meat from each side of the rear portion of the body.

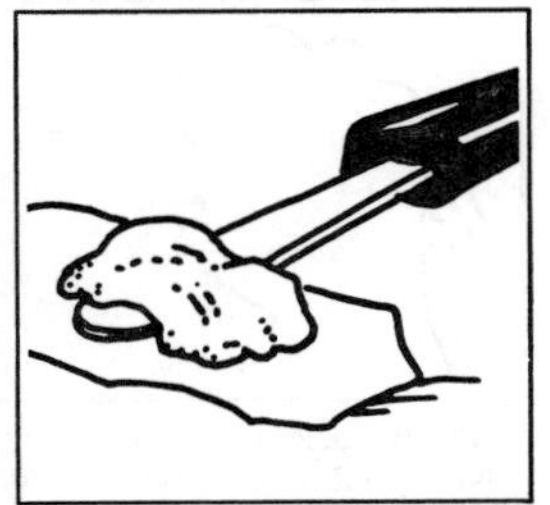

5. Remove the remainder of the meat by prying upward with the knife.

HOW TO CLEAN A SHRIMP

1. With a sharp knife, make a shallow cut along the back of the shrimp, from head to tail. Peel off shell, leaving the shell on the tail, if desired. To devein, hold shrimp under cold running water. The water will help rinse out the vein.

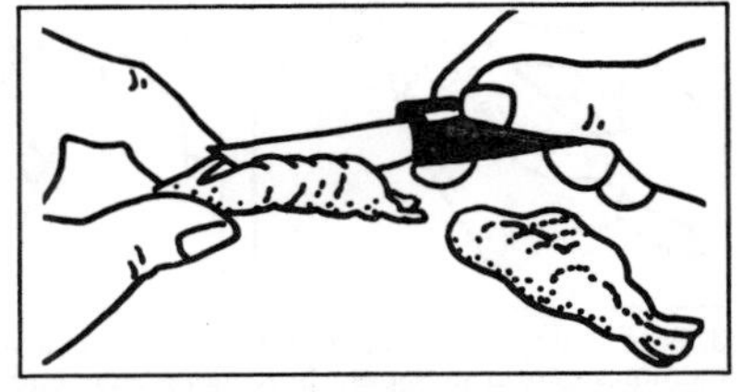

2. To butterfly, cut along the back of the shrimp, but not all the way through. Spread the halves open.

HOW TO DRESS A LOBSTER

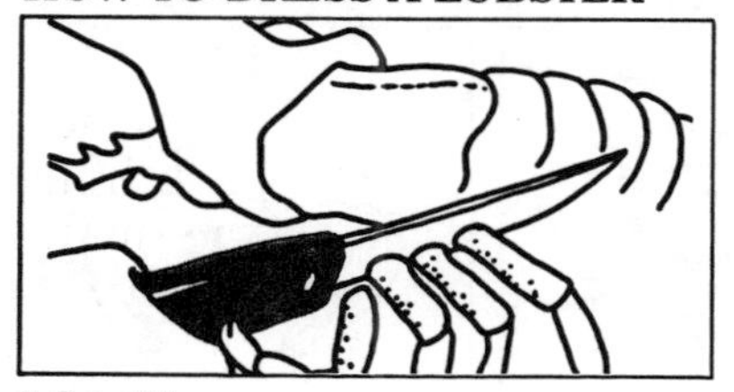

1. Cut off legs.

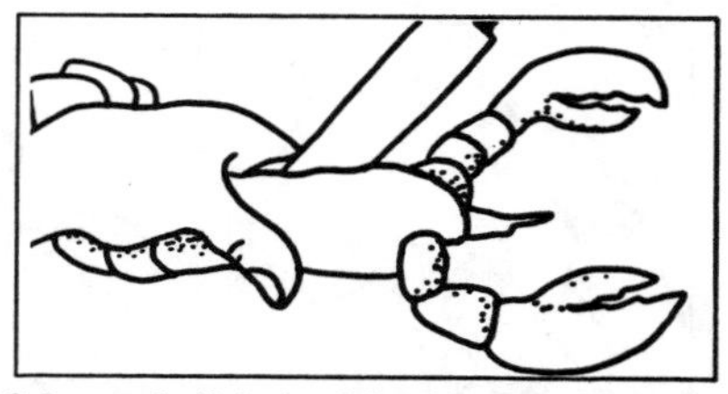

2. Insert a knife in the abdomen, and cut through the undershell toward the head, leaving back shell intact.

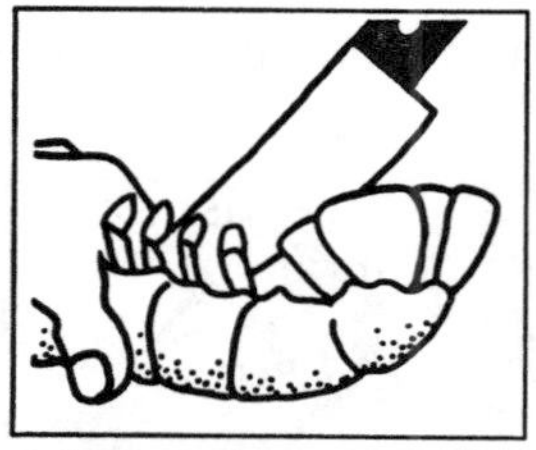

3. Cut toward the tail

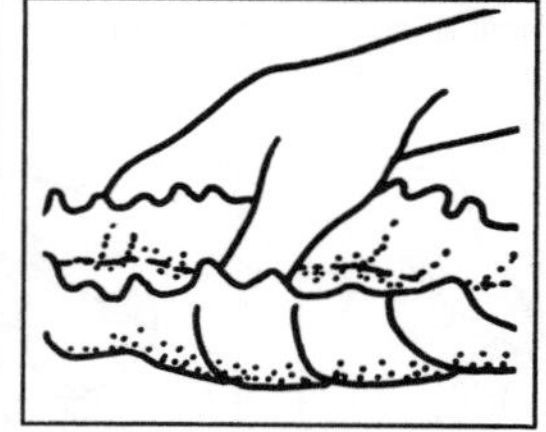

4. Press the lobster apart.

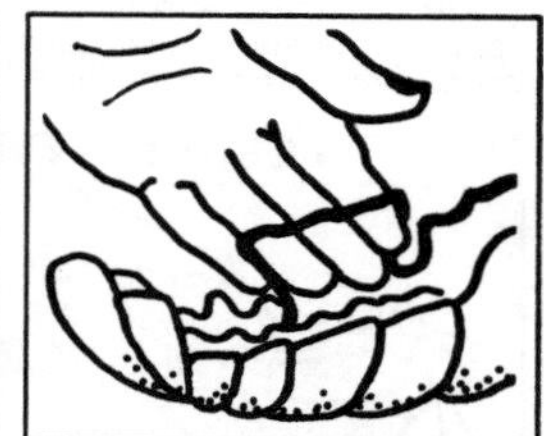

5. Remove sand sac from head; remove intestinal tract.

HOW TO DRESS A SQUID

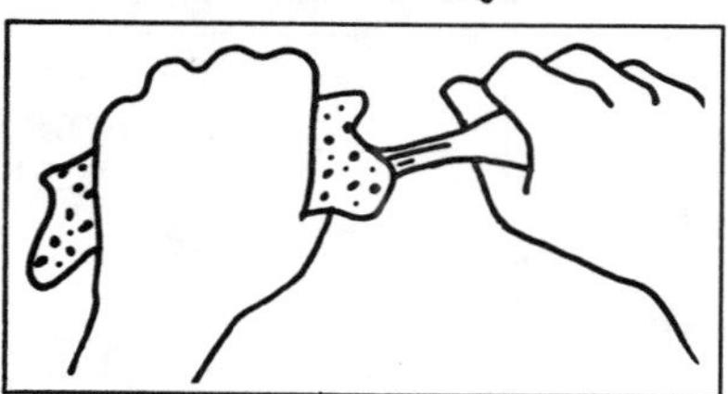

1. Pull tentacles firmly but slowly from outer body sac, leaving body intact. Intestines should come out with tentacles.

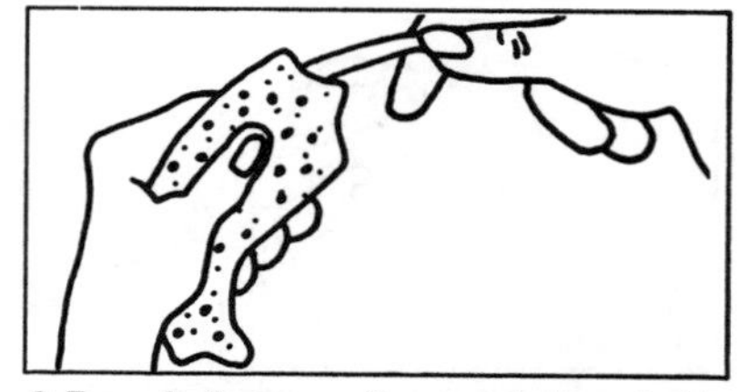

2. From body sac, pull out and discard thin, transparent quill.

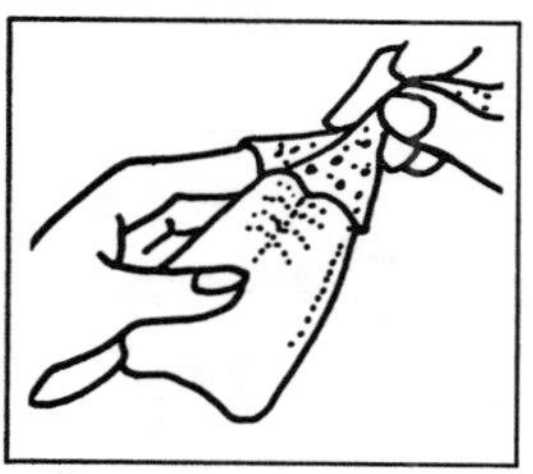

3. Peel away speckled outer membrane covering sac and fins. Turn body sac inside out, and rinse.

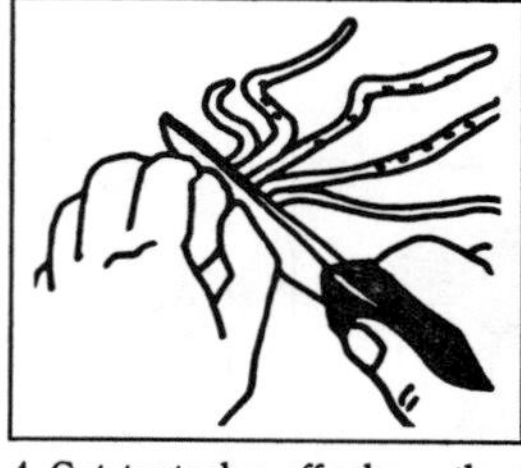

4. Cut tentacles off where they join head, and discard head.

5. The tube may be stuffed or sliced, and the tentacles chopped.

AFTER THE CATCH: THE CARE AND HANDLING OF SPORT-CAUGHT FISH

The best meals are often enjoyed with your own seafood caught on sportfishing trips. A favorite meal on the beach may be barbecued salmon, corn on the cob, coleslaw and watermelon. Sportfishing trips can be elaborate or simple. Whether you catch six Rainbow trout, several freshwater bass, a 30-pound halibut, or a Coho salmon, planning ahead for the care and handling of your catch is crucial.

- Bleed fish immediately while fish is still alive. Blood causes rapid deterioration in quality. To bleed fish, cut several gill arches to promote rapid bleeding.
- Remove gills. After the blood stops flowing out of the gills pull them out and discard them. Gills can be an area for spoilage.
- Remove all entrails and blood and wash body cavity thoroughly with cold water.
- Keep your catch cool on ice. Fill body and gill cavity with ice. Fish and shellfish held at 32° F can last at least 7 days.
- Position fish so it **does not** sit in the water from melted ice. Drain water as it accumulates.
- Surround fish in ice. Ice is your best friend for keeping fish in prime condition.

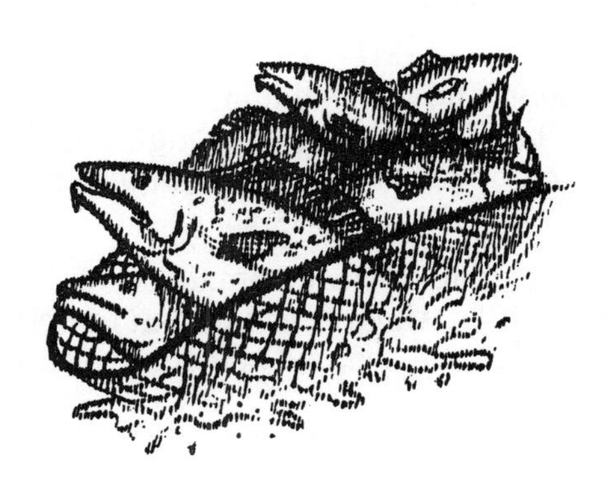

HOW TO COOK SEAFOOD TO PERFECTION

BASIC SEAFOOD COOKING METHODS ... the light and lean way!

The following preparation methods serve as basic guidelines for preparing seafood to delicious perfection while still keeping calories at a minimum.

Bake

Place seafood in baking dish. Add sauce or topping to keep moist. Cover and bake at 400° to 450° until done.

Broil

Place seafood in broiler pan. Brush with marinade, sauce, small amount of margarine, lemon juice or other topping. Flavor as desired with herbs and spices such as pepper and dill weed. Broil 4 to 5 inches from heat source without turning. Cook until done.

Poach

Estimate amount of liquid needed to cover seafood in poaching pan or saucepan. Suggested liquids include seasoned water, chicken broth, tomato juice or wine. Season liquid as desired. Bring to boil; cover and simmer about 10 minutes. Add seafood and bring to boil. Reduce heat and simmer until done.

Steam

Place seafood on a steaming rack, set two inches above boiling liquid, in deep pot. Season as desired. Cover tightly. Reduce heat and steam until done.

Grill or Barbecue

Place seafood on lightly-oiled grill. Baste with sauce or marinade as desired. Turn halfway through cooking time. Continue to baste throughout cooking time. Cook until done.

Sauté

Use non-stick pan or heat a small amount of margarine or oil with liquid such as wine, in frying pan or sauté pan. Add vegetables as desired. Add seafood and sauté over medium heat until done.

HOW TO COOK FISH

Perfectly cooked fish is moist and has a delicate flavor. There's no secret about cooking fish properly. Fish is done when the flesh has just begun to turn from translucent to opaque (or white) and is firm but still moist. It should flake when tested with a fork.

THE 10-MINUTE RULE FOR FISH

The 10-Minute Rule is one way to cook fish by conventional methods (but not deep-frying or microwaving). It can be used for baking (at 400° to 450°), grilling, broiling, poaching, steaming and sautéing. Here is how to use the 10-Minute Rule:

- Measure the fish at its thickest point. If the fish is stuffed or rolled, measure it after stuffing or rolling.
- Cook fish about 10 minutes per inch, turning it halfway through the cooking time. For example, a 1-inch fish steak should be cooked 5 minutes on each side for a total of 10 minutes. Pieces less than 1/2 inch thick do not have to be turned over. Test for doneness. Flake with a fork. Fish should reach an internal temperature of 145°.
- Add 5 minutes to the total cooking time for fish cooked in foil or in sauce.
- Double the cooking time for frozen fish that has not been defrosted. Use this rule as a general guideline since fillets often don't have uniform thickness.

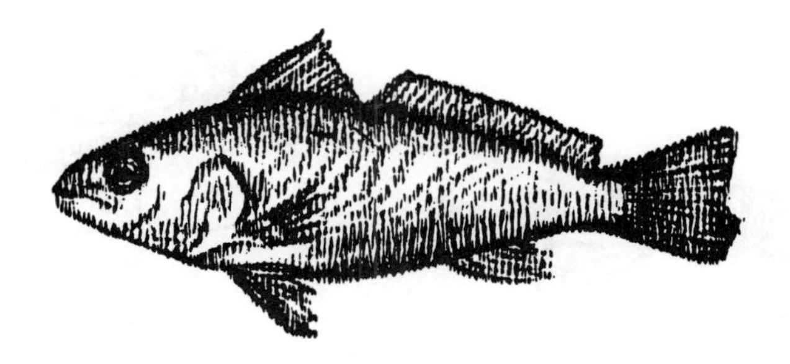

HOW TO COOK SHELLFISH

Shellfish, like fish, should not be overcooked. If it's cooked too long, it becomes tough and dry and loses much of its fine flavor.

Some shellfish and all surimi seafood are already cooked when purchased. Merely heat them for a few minutes until they are uniformly heated.

Cook raw shellfish, shucked or in the shell, very lightly. You can actually see when shellfish is cooked:

- Raw shrimp turn pink and firm. Cooking time depends on the size. It takes from 3 to 5 minutes to boil or steam 1 pound of medium-sized shrimp in the shell.
- Shucked shellfish (oysters, clams and mussels) become plump and opaque. The edges of oysters start to curl. Overcooking causes them to shrink and toughen.
- Oysters, clams and mussels, in the shell, open. Remove them one-by-one as they open and continue cooking until all are done.
- Scallops turn milky-white or opaque and firm. Sea scallops take 3 to 4 minutes to cook through; the smaller bay scallops take 30 to 60 seconds.
- Boiled lobster turns bright red. Allow 18 to 20 minutes per pound, starting from the time the water comes back to the boil. Broiled split lobster takes about 15 minutes.
- Cooking time for crabs depends on the type and preparation method. Sautéed or deep-fried soft-shell crabs take about 3 minutes each. Steamed hard-shell blue crabs or rock crabs take about 25 to 30 minutes for a large pot of them.

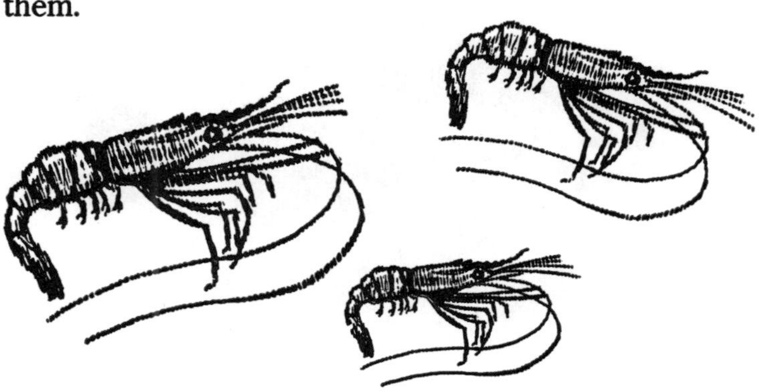

HOW TO MICROWAVE SEAFOOD

Seafood cooks perfectly in the microwave oven. It remains tender, moist and flavorful. Almost all kinds of seafood can be prepared in the microwave oven. However, there are many microwave ovens on the market and they vary in power. You may need to experiment to find the right cooking time for a particular recipe.

Watch closely when you try a new recipe for the first time. If a range of times is given, start with the shortest one. You can always put the dish back in the oven and cook it a little longer, but you cannot turn the clock back if it has cooked too long. Write the correct time down on the recipe for future reference.

Split-second timing is the secret to cooking seafood in the microwave. Seafood cooked by microwave is done when the flesh has just begun to change from translucent to opaque or white and when it is firm but still moist. Seafood will continue to cook after it has been removed from the microwave, so take the dish out before it looks done–when the outer edges are opaque with the center still slightly translucent. Allow the fish to stand, covered, for a few minutes before serving to complete cooking.

How to Microwave Fish

- Use a shallow microwave-proof dish to hold the fish.
- Shield the head and tail of a whole fish with aluminum foil to guard against excess drying. (It is safe to use small amounts of foil in newer microwave ovens.) Make several diagonal slashes through the skin of the fish to prevent it from bursting.
- Arrange fillets in a dish with the thicker parts pointing outward and the thinner parts toward the center of the dish. Rolled fillets cook more evenly by microwave than flat fillets.
- Cover the dish with plastic wrap and vent by turning back a corner.
- Allow 3 to 6 minutes per pound of boneless fish cooked on high (100% power) as a guide. Rotate the dish halfway through the cooking time.
- Fish may also be poached in a liquid in the microwave. Bring the liquid (fish stock or water and wine) to a boil, then add fish. Cover with plastic wrap and cook as described above.
- Cook side dishes first and keep them covered while cooking the fish. They will retain heat longer than fish.

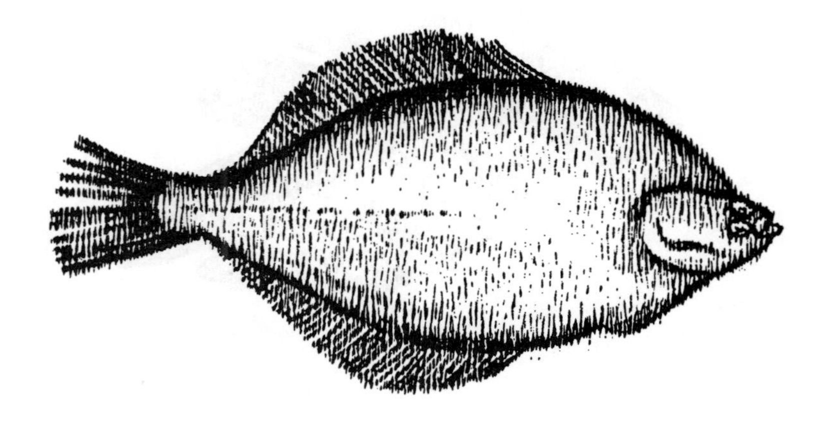

How to Microwave Shellfish

- Arrange a single layer of shellfish in a shallow dish and cover with plastic wrap turned back at one corner for venting.
- Allow 2 to 3 minutes per pound of thawed, shucked shellfish cooked on high (100% power). Stir and rotate halfway through the cooking time. Allow to stand for one-third of the cooking time after removing from the oven. (For example, if you cook 1/2 pound of shucked shellfish for 1 minute and 30 seconds, allow it to stand for 30 seconds before serving.) Be careful not to overcook.
- Place clams, mussels or oysters in the shell in a single layer in a shallow dish. Cover with plastic wrap, venting at one corner. Cook for 2 to 3 minutes on high (100% power). Check and remove pieces as they open. Continue until all have opened. 1 pound will take 12 to 15 minutes.

CREATIVE IDEAS TO INTRODUCE SEAFOOD
TO HESITANT FAMILY AND FRIENDS!

- Modify a favorite family recipe. If your family enjoys teriyaki chicken, they will love teriyaki fish.
- Serve your family a meal of their favorite dishes but include a small portion of seafood, too.
- For those who are wary of fish bones, buy boneless fish fillets or have your seafood service person debone fish for you. Any fish can be made boneless by pulling out the bones with a needle-nose plier, just like they do in restaurants. Common boneless varieties are orange roughy, Alaskan jumbo cod, monkfish, crab, imitation crab, and scallops.
- Try new and delicious recipes that include seafood, such as "Italian Cioppino" (see page 93), that have familiar wonderful flavors that kids love.
- For the steak and potato lover, start with firm-fleshed seafood species such as halibut, swordfish, fresh tuna or shark.

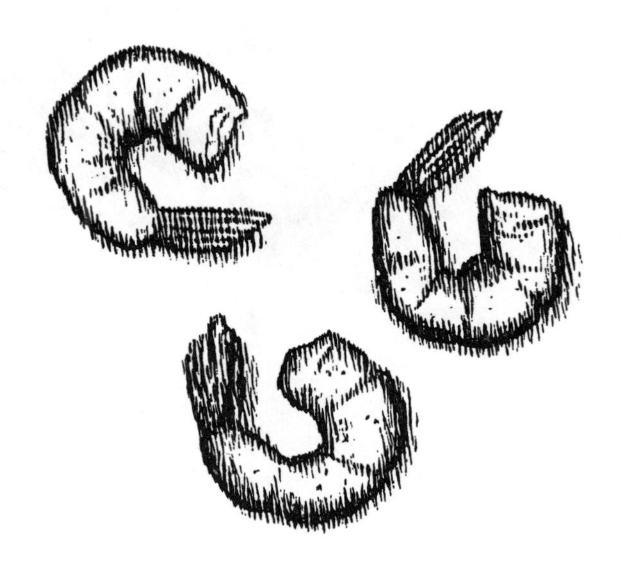

TEN "MUST-TRY" RECIPES

Listed are ten recipes that are especially good. Try them out on your family and friends! The recipes selected here are easy to prepare and are an excellent beginning for the cook who is unfamiliar with seafood cookery or for the experienced cook who wants a new sure-fire seafood recipe!

Italian Cioppino, page 93

Steamed Mussels or Clams, page 168

Hot Seafood Salad, page 76

Easy Shrimp and Pea Salad, page 83

Sesame Prawns, page 228

Orange Roughy with Oriental Sauce, page 203

Poached Cod with Herbs, page 115

Halibut in Tarragon, page 199

Sautéed Orange Roughy, page 221

Broiled Salmon Steaks with Herb Sauce, page 141

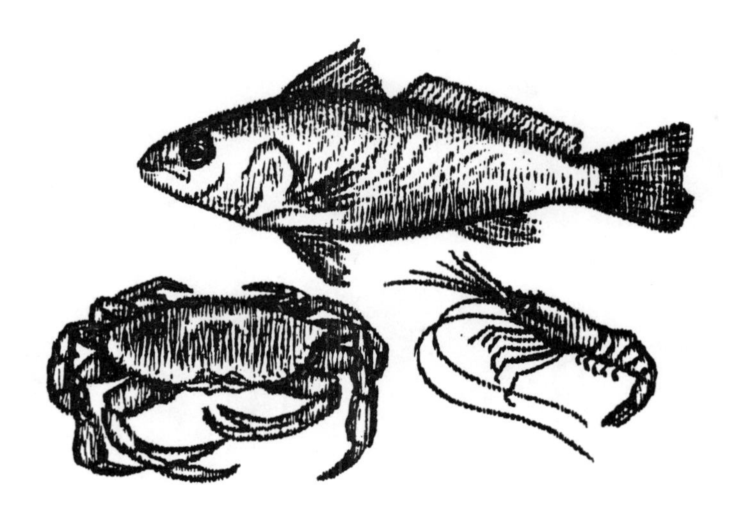

CHAPTER TWO

GREAT BEGINNINGS

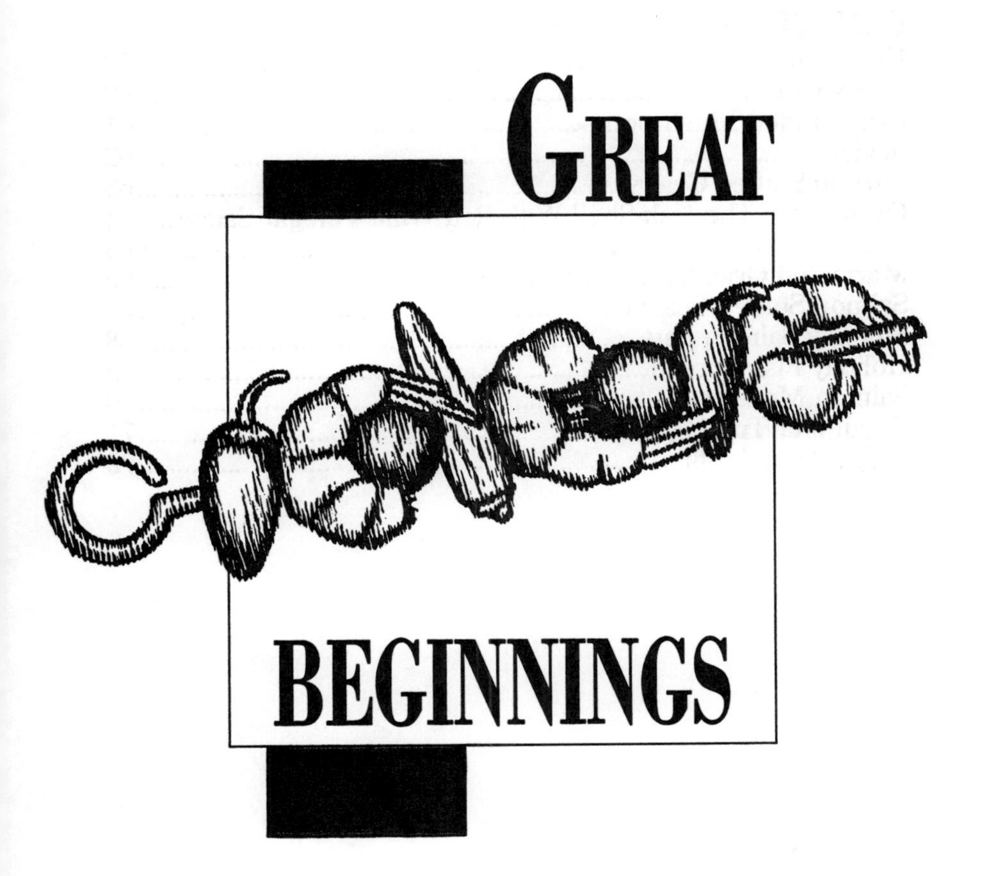

CHAPTER 2

GREAT BEGINNINGS

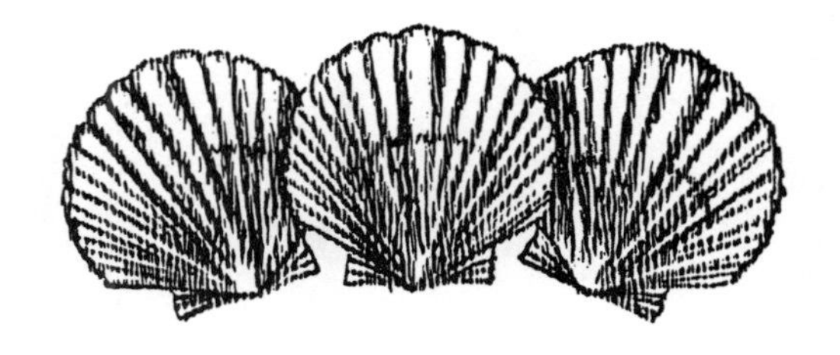

HOT CRAB SPREAD

8 oz. lite cream cheese
2 cups non-fat quark
¼ cup lemon juice
¼ cup skim milk
½ teaspoon each dried basil, marjoram, oregano and thyme
¼ teaspoon garlic powder
1 lb. imitation crab flakes

In large bowl mix cream cheese and quark until smooth. Gradually add lemon juice and milk and blend. Stir in remaining ingredients. Pour in quiche dish or pie pan. Cover. Bake at 350° for 15 minutes or until hot. Serve with crackers and vegetable tray. Makes about 4 cups.

19 calories per tablespoon | *.5 gram fat per tablespoon*
68 mg sodium per tablespoon | *8 mg cholesterol per tablespoon*

Substitutions: *cooked shrimp meat, crab meat*

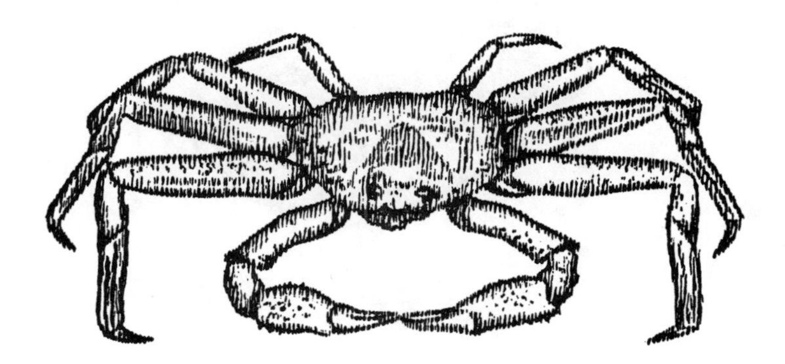

LIVELY CRAB DIP

1 cup non-fat quark or
low fat cottage cheese, processed
3 oz. lite cream cheese
2 tablespoons lite mayonnaise
1 tablespoon dried minced onion
¼ teaspoon garlic powder
4 - 6 dashes hot pepper sauce (Tabasco)
½ lb. imitation crab flakes

Combine all ingredients except crab in a bowl. Stir until smooth. Blend in crab. Refrigerate 2-3 hours to blend flavors before serving. Serve on crackers or snack-size bread. Makes about 3 cups dip.

11 calories per tablespoon *.5 gram fat per tablespoon*
45 mg sodium per tablespoon *5 mg cholesterol per tablespoon*

Substitutions: *cooked, flaked fish, crab meat*

CRAB STUFFED MUSHROOMS

2 tablespoons margarine
4 tablespoons green onion, finely chopped
1 clove garlic, finely minced
1½ cups imitation crab flakes
2 tablespoons part-skim ricotta cheese
1 teaspoon lemon juice
2 tablespoons dry bread crumbs
white pepper
¼ cup water
18-24 large mushroom tops

Melt margarine in 8 to 10-inch skillet over moderate heat. Sauté green onion and garlic, stirring constantly, for 2 minutes. Stir in crab, ricotta cheese, lemon juice, bread crumbs and white pepper and toss with onion for 10 seconds. Lightly oil a 9x13-inch pan and add ¼ cup water. Place mushroom tops in one layer and spoon on crab filling. Cover and bake at 350° for 15-20 minutes until mushrooms are tender when pierced with knife and filling is bubbly. Serve on platter. Makes 6 servings.

110 calories per serving *5 grams fat per serving*
385 mg sodium per serving *25 mg cholesterol per serving*

Substitutions: *crab meat, cooked shrimp meat*

SEVICHE

1½ lbs. imitation crab
¾ cup fresh lime juice
2 tomatoes, diced
½ cup red onion, grated
pepper to taste
¼ teaspoon garlic powder
¼ cup olive oil
3 tablespoons cilantro, finely chopped

Dice imitation crab and cover with lime juice for 30 minutes. Drain. Mix crab with remaining ingredients. Serve very cold in prechilled cocktail glasses. Garnish with parsley. Makes 8 servings.

150 calories per serving *7 grams fat per serving*
500 mg sodium per serving *40 mg cholesterol per serving*

Substitutions: *crab meat, cooked shrimp meat*

Imitation crab and other similar products are made from natural seafood. These products are made from white fish, usually Pacific pollock, which is deboned, minced, washed, and reduced to a paste, called surimi. Meat or juices of crab may be mixed into the surimi. It is then shaped to resemble crab legs or flakes. Their use is common in some restaurants in dishes such as seafood salads.

SHRIMP STUFFED CELERY

1 - 7 oz. can shrimp
⅓ cup lite mayonnaise
1½ tablespoons lemon juice
2 tablespoons parsley flakes
1½ tablespoons onion, finely chopped
⅓ cup crushed unsweetened pineapple
2 tablespoons walnuts, chopped
¼ teaspoon salt (optional)
4 drops hot pepper sauce (Tabasco)
6 celery stalks
dash paprika

In a 1-quart bowl, combine all ingredients except celery and paprika. Mix until well blended. Fill celery sticks with mixture. Sprinkle with paprika. Cut into 2-inch lengths. Makes 8-10 servings as an appetizer.

70 calories per serving *2 grams fat per serving*
145 mg sodium per serving *50 mg cholesterol per serving*

Substitutions: *cooked shrimp meat, crab meat, imitation crab*

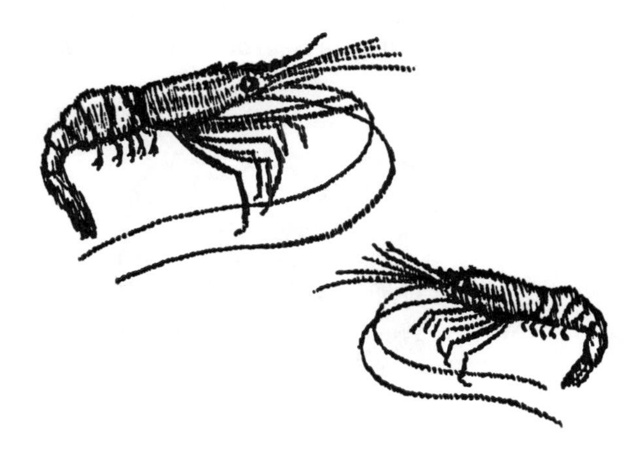

OYSTERS ON THE HALF SHELL WITH RED WINE VINEGAR SAUCE

24 oysters in the shell

Sauce:
5 oz. red wine vinegar
2 tablespoons olive oil
3 tablespoons shallots or green onion, finely minced
1 tablespoon parsley, finely minced

Clean oysters by scrubbing under cold running water. Open with an oyster knife. Free the oyster and leave on the half shell. To make sauce: mix vinegar, oil and onion. Garnish with parsley. Serve oysters with sauce on the side. Makes 8 servings.

65 calories per serving *4 grams fat per serving*
30 mg sodium per serving *25 mg cholesterol per serving*

Only eat oysters harvested from state approved beaches or from reputable seafood suppliers.

SKEWERED SCALLOPS

1 lb. scallops
2 large green peppers
1 pint cherry tomatoes

Sauce:
⅓ cup lemon juice
3 tablespoons honey
3 tablespoons prepared mustard
2 tablespoons vegetable oil
1½ teaspoons curry powder

Cut large scallops in half. Cut green peppers into 1-inch squares. Alternate scallops, tomatoes and green pepper on 20 skewers or round toothpicks, approximately 3 inches long. Place kabobs on lightly-oiled broiler pan. To make sauce: combine sauce ingredients. Brush kabobs with sauce. Broil about 4 inches from source of heat for 2 - 3 minutes. Turn carefully and brush with sauce. Broil about 1 - 2 minutes longer, basting once. Makes approximately 20 kabobs.

40 calories per kabob *2 grams fat per kabob*
70 mg sodium per kabob *8 mg cholesterol per kabob*

Substitutions: *peeled and deveined shrimp (prawns), halibut, monkfish, swordfish (cut into 1-inch cubes)*

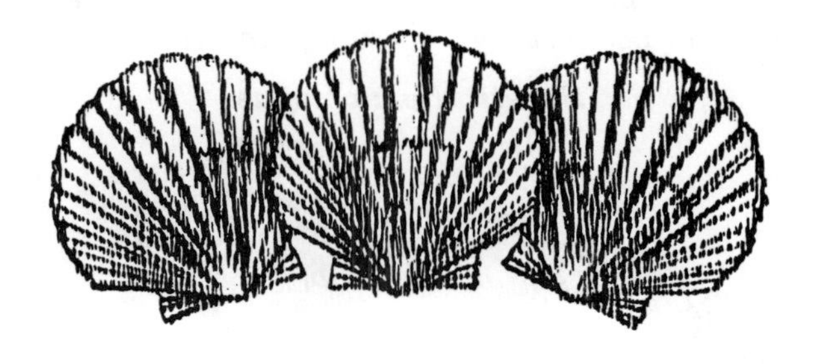

MARINATED ORIENTAL SQUID (CALAMARI)

"Great For A Party"

1 lb. squid steaks
2 quarts water
2 bay leaves
¼ teaspoon salt
½ cup white vinegar
¼ cup sugar
¼ cup vegetable oil
2 tablespoons light soy sauce
2 tablespoons lemon juice
¼ cup green onion, sliced
1 teaspoon garlic powder
2 tablespoons fresh ginger, grated
sesame seeds
Japanese horseradish

Cut squid steaks into ¼-inch strips. Prepare squid by boiling in water, bay leaves and salt for 10 minutes. Cool. In medium bowl, combine vinegar, sugar, oil, wine, light soy sauce, lemon juice, onion, garlic powder and ginger. Place squid into bowl. Let stand several hours or overnight to blend flavors. To serve, drain squid and place on a platter with a bowl each of marinade sauce, sesame seeds and Japanese horseradish. Dip squid into sauce, then seeds and horseradish. Makes 8 servings.

140 calories per serving *7.5 grams fat per serving*
290 mg sodium per serving *130 mg cholesterol per serving*

Substitution: *octopus*

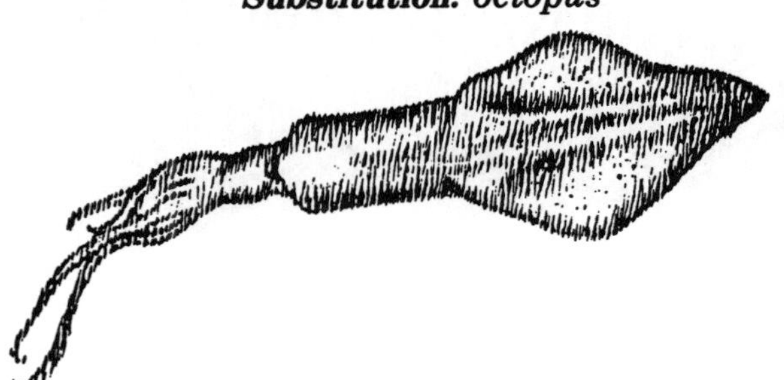

SALMON STUFFED SEASHELLS

1 - 8 oz. package conch-shaped pasta shells
¼ teaspoon salt
2 eggs, beaten
2 cups part-skim ricotta cheese
½ cup green pepper, finely chopped
¼ cup onion, finely chopped
¼ cup fresh parsley, finely chopped
¼ cup skim milk
½ teaspoon lemon peel, finely grated
1 - 15½ oz. can salmon, drained and flaked
⅓ cup dry bread crumbs
⅓ cup Parmesan cheese, grated
2 tablespoons margarine, melted

Cook pasta, uncovered, in a large amount of boiling, salted water until tender; drain and set aside. In a medium bowl combine eggs, ricotta cheese, green pepper, onion, chopped parsley, milk and lemon peel. Stir in salmon. Spoon mixture into cooked shells. Place shells, filled side up, in a 9x13-inch baking dish. Add 2 tablespoons water to dish. Cover and bake at 350° for 30 minutes. Combine the bread crumbs, Parmesan cheese and melted margarine; sprinkle over shells. Bake, uncovered, 5 minutes more. Serve hot. Garnish with lemon and lime wedges and parsley, if desired. Makes 30 appetizers.

92 calories per appetizer | *3.8 grams fat per appetizer*
137 mg sodium per appetizer | *34 mg cholesterol per appetizer*

Substitutions: *imitation crab, canned water-packed tuna*

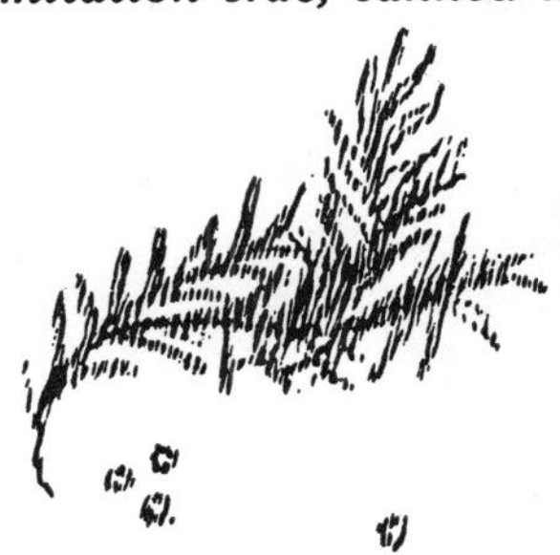

SMOKEY SALMON PATÉ

1 - 15½ oz. can salmon
⅔ cup low fat cottage cheese, blended, or non-fat quark
¼ teaspoon liquid smoke flavoring
1 tablespoon lemon juice
2 tablespoons onion, minced
2 tablespoons ripe olives, finely chopped
1 teaspoon Worcestershire sauce
½ teaspoon paprika

Drain salmon and chop very fine or mash with a fork. Press cottage cheese through a sieve or blend smooth and combine with salmon and remaining ingredients. Mix well. Cover and chill for at least one hour. Serve with melba toast or rye bread. Makes 2½ cups or 40 appetizers.

20 calories per serving *1 gram fat per serving*
75 mg sodium per serving *6 grams cholesterol per serving*

HOLIDAY FISH SPREAD

1 - 15½ oz. can salmon, drained
8 oz. low fat cottage cheese or non-fat quark
2 tablespoons onion, finely chopped
1 tablespoon parsley, minced
½ cup almonds, finely chopped
1 teaspoon liquid smoke
¼ teaspoon pepper
1 tablespoon lemon juice
1 teaspoon horseradish
¼ teaspoon garlic powder
2 tablespoons red or green pepper, finely chopped

Blend cottage cheese until smooth using a food processor or blender. Add remaining ingredients and process. Chill several hours or overnight. Excellent as a spread on dark rye bread with cucumber slices. Serve in stuffed celery sticks or as a dip for raw vegetables. Makes about 3 cups or 48 appetizer sandwiches.

29 calories per tablespoon *1.6 grams fat per tablespoon*
65 mg sodium per tablespoon *10 mg cholesterol per tablespoon*

Substitutions: *any cooked, flaked fish*

Quark is a delicate, soft white cheese; a cross between cream cheese and yogurt. It is also known as quarg, hoop or farmer's cheese. Quark is very popular in Germany, Holland and Switzerland. Non-fat quark is low in calories and fat. (Calories - 70 cal./½ cup, Fat - 0 grams/½ cup)

SALMON MOUSSE

3 egg whites
¼ teaspoon cream of tartar
2 envelopes unflavored gelatin
¾ cup cold water
1 - 15½ oz. can salmon
1 cup low fat cottage cheese, small curd or non-fat quark
½ cup plain low fat yogurt
¾ cup green onion, minced
½ cup celery, chopped
1 tablespoon lemon juice
1 teaspoon horseradish
¼ teaspoon cayenne pepper
¼ teaspoon hot pepper sauce (Tabasco)
non-stick cooking spray
radishes, cucumber slices and lemon wedges for garnish

Place egg whites and cream of tartar in a small bowl. Let warm to room temperature. In a small saucepan sprinkle gelatin over cold water; let stand 5 minutes to soften. Stir over low heat until gelatin is completely dissolved. Remove from heat; turn into medium bowl; cool to room temperature. Drain salmon. In food processor or with electric blender process salmon, cottage cheese, yogurt and horseradish until smooth and pastelike — about 1 minute. Turn into bowl with gelatin. Stir green onion, celery, lemon juice, cayenne, and Tabasco into salmon mixture. Beat egg whites to stiff peaks and fold into salmon mixture. Spray a 1-quart fish mold with non-stick cooking spray. Turn salmon mixture into mold. Refrigerate 3-4 hours or until firm. Unmold mixture. To garnish: cut several radishes into thin slices; place 2 slices for eyes; cut remaining slices in quarters; overlap on surface of salmon mousse to simulate scales. Garnish serving plate with additional radishes, cucumber slices and lemon wedges. Makes 10 servings.

80 calories per serving — *2.3 grams fat per serving*
210 mg sodium per serving — *65 mg cholesterol per serving*

Substitutions: *any cooked, flaked fish*

CUCUMBER TUNA SPREAD

1 - 6½ oz. can water-packed tuna
2 cups low fat cottage cheese or non-fat quark
¼ cup green onion, finely chopped
¼ cup green pepper, finely chopped
2 tablespoons pimiento, finely chopped
1 tablespoon Worcestershire sauce
celery, green pepper or cucumber

Drain and flake fish; place in a medium bowl. Add blended or processed cottage cheese, onion, green pepper, pimiento and Worcestershire sauce; mix well. Cover and chill 1-2 hours. Serve as an appetizer and spread on celery chunks, green pepper wedges or cucumber slices, etc., or use as a salad to stuff green pepper halves or tomatoes. Can also be used as a topping for baked potatoes. Makes 6 salad servings or 48 appetizers.

112 calories per serving *2.5 grams fat per serving*
450 mg sodium per serving *20 mg cholesterol per serving*

Substitutions: *canned salmon, any cooked, flaked fish*

JUDY'S TUNA PUFFS

2 - 6½ oz. cans water-packed tuna
2 cups celery, finely chopped
¼ cup mayonnaise
¼ cup plain low fat yogurt
2 tablespoons onion, finely chopped
2 tablespoons sweet pickle, chopped
Puff Shells

Drain and flake fish. Combine all ingredients except puff shells. Mix thoroughly. Cut tops from puff shells. Fill each puff shell with approximately 2 teaspoonfuls of salad. Makes approximately 72 puffs.

Puff Shells
1 cup boiling water
½ cup margarine
1 cup flour
4 eggs

Combine water and margarine in a saucepan and bring to a boil. Add flour all at one time and stir vigorously until mixture forms a ball and leaves the sides of the pan. Remove from heat. Add eggs, one at a time, beating thoroughly after each addition. Continue beating until a stiff dough is formed. Drop by level teaspoonfuls on a cooking sheet. Bake at 450° for 10 minutes. Reduce heat to 350° and continue baking for about 10 minutes longer. Let cool completely before filling. Makes approximately 72 puff shells.

38 calories per filled puff *2.3 grams fat per filled puff*
50 mg sodium per filled puff *20 mg cholesterol per filled puff*

Substitutions: *canned salmon, crab meat, cooked shrimp meat*

C H A P T E R T H R E E

SALADS

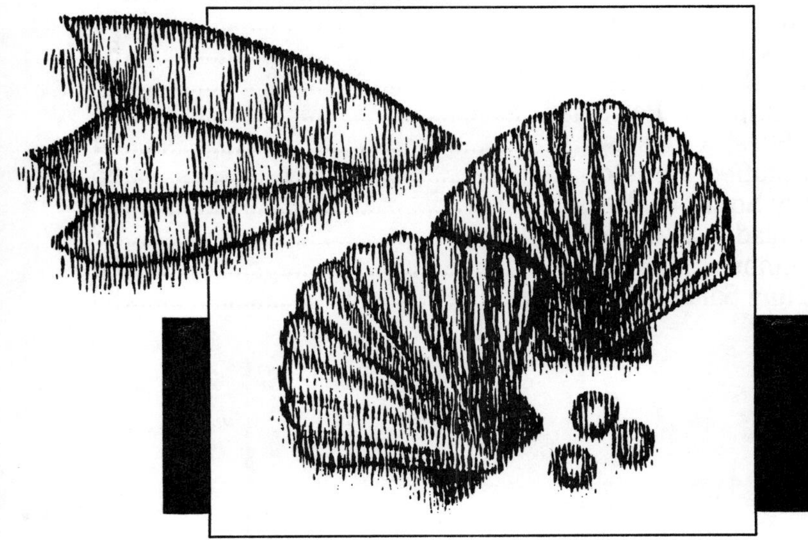

CHAPTER 3

SALADS

CRAB LOUIE

lettuce leaves
2 cups lettuce leaves, shredded
1 celery stalk, sliced
radishes, sliced
2 cups crab meat
2 hard-cooked egg whites, sliced
chives, chopped
tomato wedges
lemon wedges

Arrange lettuce leaves in a salad bowl. Place shredded lettuce over leaves. Add celery, radishes and seafood. Top with egg white slices, chives and tomato wedges. Serve with lemon wedges and Thousand Island Dressing (see page 245) on the side. Makes 4 servings.

110 calories per serving — *1.3 grams fat per serving*
265 mg sodium per serving — *90 mg cholesterol per serving*

Substitutions: *cooked shrimp meat, imitation crab*

HOT SEAFOOD SALAD

1 cup crab meat
1 green pepper, finely chopped
1 cup celery, finely chopped
1 small onion, finely chopped
1 cup toasted bread cubes
1 cup low fat cottage cheese, blended, or non-fat quark
2 tablespoons mayonnaise
2 tablespoons lemon juice
1 teaspoon Worcestershire sauce
½ cup part-skim mozzarella cheese, grated
paprika

CONVENTIONAL METHOD:
Combine all ingredients. Mix well. Pour into 1½-quart glass casserole or other baking dish. Sprinkle with paprika. Bake at 350° for 25-30 minutes.

MICROWAVE METHOD:
Place ingredients in microwave-proof container; cover. Cook at medium power for 10 minutes; turning once. Stir once. Makes 8 servings.

125 calories per serving *5 grams fat per serving*
245 mg sodium per serving *20 mg cholesterol per serving*

Substitutions: *cooked, flaked fish, imitation crab*

Serve this at your next luncheon.

SEAFOOD PEAR SALAD

1 - 16 oz. can unsweetened pear halves
¼ cup low fat cottage cheese
2 tablespoons lemon juice
8 oz. imitation crab flakes
1 green onion, chopped
lettuce leaves

Set aside 4 pear halves. Cube remaining pear halves. In medium bowl mix cottage cheese and lemon juice. Gently fold in pear cubes, crab and green onion. Spoon into reserved pear halves. Serve on lettuce. If desired, garnish with lemon wedges and radishes. Makes 4 servings.

82 calories per serving *1.1 grams fat per serving*
310 mg sodium per serving *30 mg cholesterol per serving*

Substitutions: *cooked shrimp meat, crab meat*

SHRIMP AND SPINACH SALAD WITH SUNSHINE DRESSING

Salad:
2 bunches spinach leaves
1 orange, peeled, sectioned & cut into bite-size pieces
1 cup mushrooms, sliced
¼ cup red onion, chopped
¼ cup carrot, grated
½ lb. cooked shrimp meat

Sunshine Dressing:
1 tablespoon olive oil
2 tablespoons frozen orange juice concentrate
1 tablespoon water
1 tablespoon white vinegar
dash dried tarragon
dash dried parsley
dash garlic powder
dash onion powder
dash pepper

To make salad: wash fresh spinach leaves, remove stems and pat dry. Toss spinach together with remaining salad ingredients. To make dressing: combine ingredients and mix well. Serve over salad. Garnish with cherry tomatoes or avocado slices. Makes 4 servings.

157 calories per serving *5 grams fat per serving*
165 mg sodium per serving *90 mg cholesterol per serving*

Substitutions: *lobster meat, imitation crab, crawfish tails*

PICANTE SEAFOOD SALAD

1 tablespoon olive oil
1 cup onion, chopped
1 cup green pepper, chopped
1 cup celery, chopped
1 large clove garlic, minced
¼ teaspoon cayenne pepper
2 cups tomatoes, chopped
1 bay leaf
½ teaspoon dried thyme
½ teaspoon crushed oregano leaves
¼ teaspoon crushed rosemary leaves
½ teaspoon pepper
1 cup tomato sauce
¼ lb. calico or bay scallops
½ lb. cooked shrimp meat
½ lb. dry pasta shells

Heat olive oil in non-stick skillet over medium heat. Add onion, green pepper, celery, garlic and cayenne pepper; sauté 10 minutes or until vegetables are tender-crisp, stirring occasionally. Stir in tomatoes, bay leaf, thyme, oregano, rosemary, pepper and tomato sauce. Simmer 15 minutes. Add scallops and shrimp; simmer just until scallops turn opaque and shrimp are hot. While sauce simmers, cook pasta in large pot of boiling water until done; drain. Combine sauce with hot pasta. Makes 6 servings.

275 calories per serving *2.6 grams fat per serving*
560 mg sodium per serving *60 mg cholesterol per serving*

If you can't find small bay scallops, substitute sea scallops and cut them into quarters.

CHOPPED SEAFOOD SALAD

Salad:
½ head iceberg lettuce, finely chopped
3 tablespoons green onion, finely chopped
1 medium tomato, seeded and finely chopped
1 cup celery, finely chopped
2 eggs, hard boiled, chopped
½ lb. cooked shrimp meat

Dressing:
1 tablespoon olive oil
2 teaspoons white vinegar
¼ teaspoon salt
Juice of ½ lemon
dash dried tarragon
dash dried parsley
dash garlic powder
dash onion powder
dash pepper

To make salad: in bowl, toss all salad ingredients together. To make dressing: mix ingredients together in small bowl. Pour on salad and toss. Makes 4 servings.

114 calories per serving *3.4 grams fat per serving*
146 mg sodium per serving *222 mg cholesterol per serving*

Substitutions: *lobster meat, crawfish tails, crab meat*

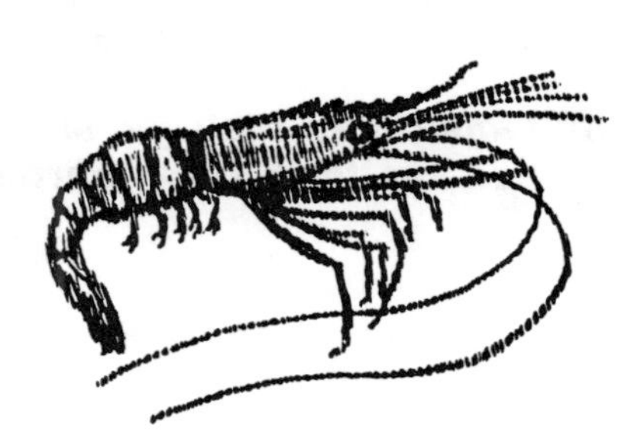

LAYERED SEAFOOD SALAD

Dressing:
1 cup plain low fat yogurt
2 tablespoons mayonnaise
½ teaspoon dried dill weed
½ teaspoon black pepper
½ teaspoon horseradish

4 cups shredded lettuce
2 green onions, finely chopped
½ cup green pepper, chopped
½ cup cucumber, sliced
½ cup frozen green peas
¼ teaspoon garlic powder
2 cups cooked shrimp meat
¼ cup part-skim mozzarella cheese, grated
tomato wedges

Combine all ingredients for dressing in a small bowl and set aside. Shred lettuce; add green onion, green pepper, cucumber and frozen peas. Toss lightly with garlic powder. Fill a 9x9-inch dish. Place shrimp evenly over salad greens. Pour dressing over all. Garnish with grated mozzarella cheese and tomato wedges. Refrigerate. Makes 4 servings.

265 calories per serving *9.7 grams fat per serving*
245 mg sodium per serving *80 mg cholesterol per serving*

Substitutions: *crab meat, canned water-packed tuna, canned salmon*

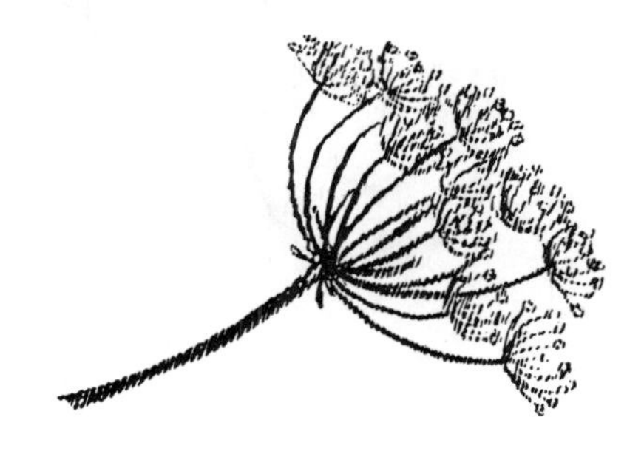

ISLAND FRESH CUCUMBER SALAD

2 medium cucumbers or 1 English cucumber, peeled and thinly sliced
½ cup white onion, thinly sliced
½ cup white vinegar
¼ teaspoon salt
dash of pepper
½ cup canned evaporated skim milk
1 teaspoon sugar
½ lb. cooked shrimp meat

Place cucumber and onion slices in a large bowl. Add vinegar, salt and pepper. Let marinate in refrigerator for 20-30 minutes. Stir occasionally. Drain vinegar from salad. Pour milk and sprinkle sugar over salad and toss. Mix in shrimp meat just before serving. Save some shrimp to garnish top of salad. Makes 4 servings.

93 calories per serving *1 gram fat per serving*
230 mg sodium per serving *91 mg cholesterol per serving*

Substitutions: *imitation crab, crab meat*

EASY SHRIMP AND PEA SALAD

1 - 16 oz. package frozen peas
1 teaspoon dried dill weed
¼ cup red onion, chopped
1 cup cooked shrimp (prawns), peeled and deveined
2 tablespoons mayonnaise
½ cup plain low fat yogurt

Mix all ingredients together. This salad is a wonderful and easy addition to any meal. Makes 8 servings.

100 calories per serving *3.3 grams fat per serving*
70 mg sodium per serving *40 mg cholesterol per serving*

Substitutions: *imitation crab, crab meat*

An easy, last minute idea for a family get-together.

GARDEN FRESH COLESLAW

1 cup cooked shrimp meat
2 cups cabbage, grated
2 teaspoons onion, finely chopped
½ cup green pepper, finely chopped
½ cup carrots, grated

Dressing:
½ cup plain low fat yogurt
⅛ teaspoon dry mustard
⅛ teaspoon pepper
1 tablespoon cider vinegar
1 tablespoon sugar

Combine shrimp, cabbage, onion, green pepper and carrots and toss together. Combine ingredients for dressing and stir. Add dressing to vegetables and mix well. Serve on a bed of lettuce with tomato wedges. Makes 4 servings.

85 calories per serving *1 gram fat per serving*
85 mg sodium per serving *50 mg cholesterol per serving*

Substitutions: *imitation crab, crab meat*

SHRIMP STUFFED TOMATO

¾ cup celery, diced
1½ cups cooked shrimp meat
¼ teaspoon pepper
2 tablespoons mayonnaise
4 ripe tomatoes
4 large lettuce leaves
1 green pepper, sliced into rings
4 radishes, cut into roses
plain low fat yogurt
parsley sprigs and paprika to garnish

In a small mixing bowl, combine celery, shrimp, pepper and mayonnaise. Toss gently until the shrimp and celery are coated with mayonnaise. Cut each tomato into five lengthwise sections, leaving them intact at the stem end. Place each on a bed of lettuce that has been arranged on a salad plate. Spread the tomato sections apart and stuff each tomato with the shrimp salad mixture. Top each with a green pepper ring. To garnish place a spoonful of yogurt on top of each salad and garnish with a sprig of parsley and a radish rose. Sprinkle with paprika. Chill until ready to serve. Makes 4 servings.

135 calories per serving *6.3 grams fat per serving*
120 mg sodium per serving *40 mg cholesterol per serving*

Substitutions: *crab meat, imitation crab, canned water-packed tuna*

MONTEREY SQUID (CALAMARI) SALAD

1 lb. cleaned squid mantles or steaks
1 tablespoon olive oil
1 teaspoon Dijon mustard
3 cloves garlic, minced
dash cayenne pepper
1 tablespoon lemon juice
⅛ teaspoon dried basil
½ teaspoon pepper
¼ red onion, thinly sliced
1 green pepper, cut into chunks
1 tablespoon parsley, chopped
2 large tomatoes, chunked

Cut squid mantles (bodies) or steaks into rounds, rings or strips. In medium skillet combine oil, mustard, garlic, cayenne, lemon juice, basil and pepper. Bring to a boil and add squid. Simmer 30 seconds or until squid turns white; remove from heat. Transfer to bowl. Stir in onion and green pepper and cover. Refrigerate 2-4 hours or overnight. Before serving, toss in parsley and tomatoes. Makes 4 servings.

160 calories per serving *4.7 grams fat per serving*
195 mg sodium per serving *265 mg cholesterol per serving*

Substitutions: *swordfish, halibut, albacore tuna*

Squid (calamari) is a free swimming mollusk. Squid range in size from 1 inch to 60 feet. The most common size found in the market is under 10 inches. Most squid in the market has been frozen. Freezing preserves quality and provides protection during handling. The flesh is firm and delicately flavored. It is very popular in Mediterranean and Oriental ethnic groups.

SPRING SALAD

1 - 7½ oz. can salmon
½ lb. fresh asparagus or broccoli

Marinade:
2 tablespoons vegetable oil
1½ tablespoons lemon juice
dash white pepper

Dressing:
½ cup plain low fat yogurt
¼ cup low fat cottage cheese
¼ teaspoon dried tarragon
parsley, chopped

1 tablespoon green onion, chopped
salad greens
tomato wedges
radish roses
celery, sliced

Chill can of salmon. Steam asparagus or broccoli just until tender-crisp. To prepare marinade: combine oil, lemon juice and pepper. Pour over asparagus or broccoli. Marinate in refrigerator 1 hour. Drain, reserving marinade. To prepare dressing: combine marinade with yogurt, cottage cheese and tarragon. Blend. Place in dish and sprinkle with parsley. Drain salmon and break into chunks with a fork. Arrange salmon and asparagus or broccoli on platter lined with green onion and crisp greens. Garnish with tomato wedges, radish roses and celery and pour dressing over salad. Makes 4 servings.

200 calories per serving *11.6 grams fat per serving*
275 mg sodium per serving *30 mg cholesterol per serving*

Substitutions: *canned water-packed tuna, cooked shrimp meat*

MAUI SALMON

1 - 15½ oz. can salmon
2 tablespoons capers
½ small red onion, thinly sliced in rings
¼ cup white wine vinegar

8 bibb lettuce heads
olives
cucumber slices
asparagus spears

Drain and flake salmon. Add capers and red onion rings. Pour vinegar over mixture and toss lightly with a fork. Chill overnight. To serve: remove center core of bibb lettuce. Place ½ cup of salmon mixture in center. Garnish with a ripe olive, cucumber slices and asparagus spears. Makes 8 servings.

190 calories per serving *8 mg fat per serving*
450 mg sodium per serving *70 mg cholesterol per serving*

CURRY TUNA SALAD

grated peel of ½ lemon
2 tablespoons lemon juice
1 tablespoon honey
¼ teaspoon ground ginger
¼ teaspoon curry powder
1 - 6½ oz. can water-packed tuna, drained and flaked
1½ cups seedless grapes, halved, or
cantaloupe balls or cubes
½ cup celery, sliced

In large bowl, combine lemon peel, lemon juice, honey, ginger, curry and garlic powder. Stir in tuna, grapes and celery; toss lightly. Serve on a bed of shredded lettuce and garnish with lemon wedges, if desired. Makes 4 servings.

120 calories per serving *.8 gram fat per serving*
190 mg sodium per serving *30 mg cholesterol per serving*

Substitutions: *crab meat, cooked shrimp meat, canned salmon*

A cool meal idea for a hot summer day.

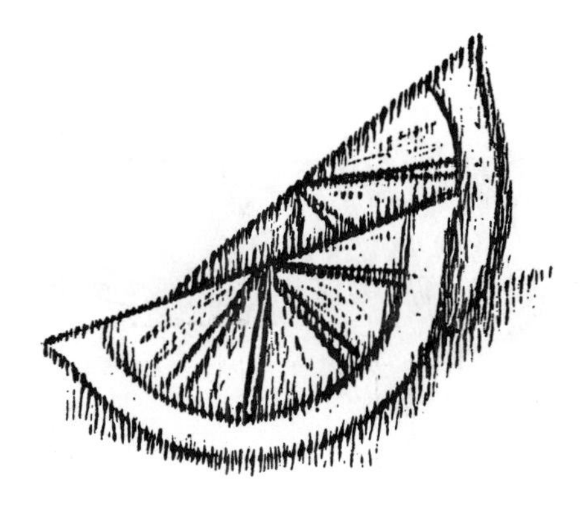

CHAPTER FOUR

SOUPS & SANDWICHES

CHAPTER 4

SOUPS AND SANDWICHES

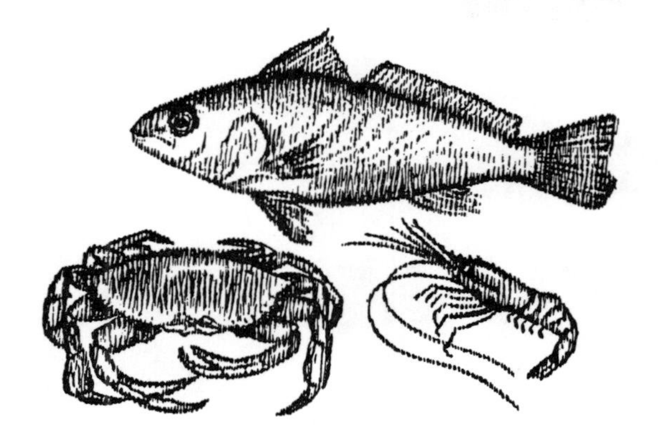

ITALIAN CIOPPINO

1½ lbs. cod
1 cup onion, chopped
2 cloves garlic, minced
1 tablespoon vegetable oil
1 - 8 oz. can tomato sauce
1 - 28 oz. can tomatoes, undrained and mashed
½ cup dry white wine or water
1 teaspoon each dried basil, thyme, marjoram and oregano
1 teaspoon sugar
1 bay leaf
¼ teaspoon pepper
4 whole cloves (optional)
1 tablespoon parsley, minced

Cut fish into ½-inch cubes and set aside. Sauté onion and garlic in oil until tender. Add tomato sauce, tomatoes, liquid and all seasonings except parsley. Let simmer 20-30 minutes, stirring occasionally. Add fish and cook until done, about 10 minutes. Add parsley. This soup is a complete meal when served with green salad and French bread. Makes 7 - 1 cup servings.

155 calories per serving *2 grams fat per serving*
405 mg sodium per serving *45 mg cholesterol per serving*

Substitutions: *chopped squid, minced clams, scallops*

Have a Cioppino party. Make base day before. Have each guest bring a quarter pound of their favorite seafood. Add to heated Cioppino base and simmer until done.

AUTUMN FISH STEW

1 lb. halibut
1 medium onion, chopped
1 tablespoon vegetable oil
1 - 28 oz. can tomatoes, undrained
2 medium potatoes, peeled and diced
½ teaspoon dried basil
¼ teaspoon pepper
¼ teaspoon sugar
1 - 10 oz. package frozen mixed vegetables

Cut fish fillets into 1-inch cubes. In 4-quart saucepan sauté onion in oil until tender. Stir in tomatoes with liquid. Add potatoes, basil, pepper and sugar and cook over high heat until boiling. Reduce heat to low; cover and simmer 20-30 minutes, stirring occasionally, until potatoes are tender. Add frozen mixed vegetables to tomato mixture and heat until just boiling. Simmer until vegetables are tender. Add fish and simmer 5 minutes or until fish flakes when tested with a fork. Makes 4 large servings.

270 calories per serving *4 grams fat per serving*
370 mg sodium per serving *45 mg cholesterol per serving*

Substitutions: *cod, haddock, monkfish*

HALIBUT VEGETABLE CHOWDER

"Kids Love It"

2 carrots, sliced
2 stalks celery, sliced diagonally
½ cup onion, chopped
2 cloves garlic, minced
2 tablespoons vegetable oil
1 - 28 oz. can tomatoes, undrained
1 cup water
3 tablespoons parsley, minced and divided
1 teaspoon chicken bouillon granules
¼ teaspoon dried thyme
¼ teaspoon dried basil
⅛ teaspoon pepper
1½ lbs. halibut

Sauté carrots, celery, onion and garlic in oil for 5 minutes. Add undrained tomatoes, water, 2 tablespoons parsley, bouillon and seasonings. Break up tomatoes with spoon. Cover and simmer 20 minutes. Cut halibut into 1-inch cubes, add to chowder. Cover and simmer 5-10 minutes or until halibut flakes when tested with a fork. Sprinkle with remaining parsley. Makes 6 servings.

196 calories per serving *6 grams fat per serving*
600 mg sodium per serving *55 mg cholesterol per serving*

Substitutions: *catfish, lingcod, salmon*

SATURDAY NIGHT SEAFOOD CHOWDER

1 lb. salmon
3 cups water
1 small onion, diced
3 medium potatoes, unpeeled, diced
2 stalks celery, chopped
2 carrots, sliced
6-8 whole allspice
1 teaspoon dried dill weed
½ teaspoon white pepper
2 - 13 oz. cans evaporated skim milk
2 tablespoons flour
1 tablespoon margarine
1 tablespoon parsley, minced

Remove skin and bones from fish. Cut fish into 1-inch cubes. Place water, onion, potatoes, celery, carrots, allspice, dill weed and white pepper into 4-quart saucepan. Cover and simmer 15 minutes. Add 3 cups milk and salmon to vegetables. Blend flour with ½ cup skim milk until smooth. Slowly stir into chowder. Simmer for 10 minutes or until fish flakes when tested with a fork. Stir gently. Dot with margarine and parsley before serving. Serve with hot French bread. Makes 6 servings.

240 calories per serving *7 grams fat per serving*
155 mg sodium per serving *50 mg cholesterol per serving*

Substitutions: *halibut, scallops, lobster meat*

NEW ENGLAND CLAM CHOWDER

1 onion, chopped
3 stalks celery, chopped
4 medium-sized potatoes, cubed
4 carrots, sliced
1 lb. clams, minced
1½ teaspoons Italian Seasoning
¼ teaspoon pepper
¼ teaspoon garlic powder
1 - 13 oz. can evaporated skim milk
1 tablespoon margarine

Place onion, celery, potatoes, carrots, clams and spices in a 3-quart saucepan. Add water to barely cover ingredients. Cover and cook over medium heat until potatoes are tender. Add evaporated skim milk and margarine and simmer. Heat thoroughly (do not boil). Serve with a roll and salad. Makes 4 servings.

Variation: Manhattan Clam Chowder
Substitute 1 - 28 oz. can of mashed whole tomatoes for evaporated milk.

280 calories per serving *4.6 grams fat per serving*
220 mg sodium per serving *45 mg cholesterol per serving*

Substitutions: *chopped squid, oysters, mussels*

CORN CHOWDER

⅔ cup onion, chopped
2 tablespoons vegetable oil
12 oz. geoduck, minced
½ cup boiling water
1½ cups potatoes, peeled and diced
¼ teaspoon pepper
1 bay leaf
1 cup skim milk
1 - 13 oz. can evaporated skim milk
1 - 17 oz. can cream-style corn
parsley, chopped

Sauté onion in oil in Dutch oven or 3-quart saucepan until tender but not brown. Add geoduck, water, potatoes, pepper and bay leaf. Cover and simmer until potatoes are tender, about 15 minutes. Remove bay leaf. Add skim and evaporated milk and corn. Heat gently (do not boil). Garnish with parsley to serve. Makes 4 servings.

350 calories per serving *5.3 grams fat per serving*
300 mg sodium per serving *30 mg cholesterol per serving*

Substitutions: *minced clams, chopped squid, oysters*

Geoduck is the largest of all American clams. Its flavor is a little richer than most clams and lends itself well to chowders.

OYSTER STEW

1 pint container oysters, undrained
1 tablespoon margarine
¼ teaspoon pepper
1 cup water
½ cup onion, finely chopped
¼ cup fresh celery leaves, chopped
1 - 13 oz. can evaporated skim milk
1 tablespoon Worcestershire sauce
2 - 3 drops hot pepper sauce (Tabasco)

Cut oysters into quarters. Melt margarine in 3-quart saucepan. Add the oysters, pepper, water, onion and celery leaves. Simmer 5 minutes. Add milk, Worcestershire sauce and hot pepper sauce. Slowly heat to steaming, but do not boil. Serve hot with green salad and roll. Makes 4 servings.

183 calories per serving *4 grams fat per serving*
215 mg sodium per serving *60 mg cholesterol per serving*

Substitutions: *scallops, monkfish medallions, lobster meat*

Start a family tradition with oyster stew for Christmas Eve dinner.

UNBELIEVABLY GOOD SQUID SOUP

1 lb. squid steaks, cubed
4 potatoes, diced
1 onion, chopped
2 stalks celery, chopped
½ green pepper, chopped
2 carrots, sliced
1 teaspoon salt-free all-purpose seasoning
4 cups water
¼ teaspoon salt
2 tablespoons flour
2 tablespoons margarine, melted
⅛ teaspoon white pepper
1 cup buttermilk
1 - 13 oz. can evaporated skim milk

Cut squid steaks into small cubes. Place squid, potatoes, onion, celery, green pepper, carrots, seasoning and water in large deep saucepan. Bring to boil. Reduce heat and simmer 20 minutes. In small bowl mix margarine, salt, white pepper and flour. Gently pour into soup mixture and stir. Simmer until soup thickens. Add buttermilk and milk just before serving. Heat thoroughly; do not boil. Makes 8 servings.

175 calories per serving *3.5 grams fat per serving*
295 mg sodium per serving *133 mg cholesterol per serving*

Substitutions: *halibut, minced clams, scallops*

LOBSTER ROLL

½ lb. lobster meat
2 tablespoons lite mayonnaise
¼ cup celery, finely chopped
4 rolls, such as French or hoagy

Mix lobster, mayonnaise and celery together. Split rolls and toast under broiler. Fill with lobster mixture and serve. Makes 4 servings.

165 calories per serving *4.5 grams fat per serving*
385 mg sodium per serving *71 mg cholesterol per serving*

Substitutions: *crab meat, cooked shrimp meat, imitation crab, crawfish tails*

ENGLISH MUFFIN SHRIMP PIZZA

"A Teenage Favorite"

6 English muffins, split or French bread, sliced

Pizza Sauce:
1 - 15 oz. can tomato sauce
1½ teaspoons Italian Seasoning
1 tablespoon dried parsley
½ teaspoon garlic powder
½ teaspoon onion powder
¼ teaspoon pepper

¾ cup onion, chopped
¾ cup mushrooms, sliced
¾ cup green pepper, chopped
½ lb. cooked shrimp meat (about 2 cups)
4 oz. part-skim mozzarella cheese, shredded

Toast English muffins. Mix ingredients for pizza sauce. Place pizza sauce on muffins. Top with onion, mushrooms and green pepper. Add shrimp. Cover with shredded cheese. Broil pizza about 3 minutes or until cheese melts. Makes 12 individual pizzas.

130 calories per pizza — *3.8 grams fat per pizza*
400 mg sodium per pizza — *30 mg cholesterol per pizza*

LUNCHBREAK TUNA SANDWICH

1 - 6½ oz. can water-packed tuna, drained and flaked
¼ cup low fat cottage cheese
1 tablespoon mayonnaise
¼ cup celery, finely chopped
2 tablespoons green onion, minced
5 radishes, diced
pepper to taste
2 tablespoons slivered almonds
3 English muffins, split and toasted

Combine all ingredients. Spread on 6 muffin halves. Serve with tomato wedges. Makes 6 sandwiches.

160 calories per sandwich *3.5 grams fat per sandwich*
245 mg sodium per sandwich *20 mg cholesterol per sandwich*

Substitutions: *canned salmon, any cooked, flaked fish*

TAKE-ME-ALONG SEAFOOD SANDWICH

1 - 6½ oz. can water-packed tuna
2 tablespoons low fat cottage cheese
1 tablespoon mayonnaise
1 tablespoon sunflower seeds, unsalted, dry roasted
1 tablespoon unsweetened pineapple, crushed
1 tablespoon celery, finely chopped
tomato slices
cucumber slices
alfalfa sprouts

Combine fish with remaining ingredients and mix. Use as a sandwich spread with tomato, cucumber slices and alfalfa sprouts on 1 slice whole grain bread or in pita bread. Serve with fresh fruit salad. Variation: serve as a cool and crunchy seafood salad on a bed of shredded lettuce. Makes 4 open-faced sandwiches.

165 calories per sandwich
5.3 grams fat per sandwich
315 mg sodium per sandwich
35 mg cholesterol per sandwich

Substitutions: *canned salmon, any cooked, flaked fish*

SALMONBURGERS

1 - 15½ oz. can salmon
1 egg
½ cup onion, chopped
1 tablespoon fresh parsley, chopped
1 tablespoon lemon juice
1 teaspoon Worcestershire sauce
¾ cup oats, quick cooking
dash pepper

Drain salmon; combine with all other ingredients. Form into 4 patties. Use a lightly-oiled non-stick skillet and fry until golden brown on both sides. Place salmon patties on bottom half of hamburger bun. Serve with lettuce, sliced tomato and pickles. For barbecuing, cook on lightly-oiled piece of foil for 6 minutes; turn and cook 6 minutes longer. Makes 4 servings.

300 calories per serving *11 grams fat per serving*
490 mg sodium per serving *130 mg cholesterol per serving*

Salmonburgers are a creative alternative to hamburgers. Enjoy this recipe at a summer barbecue.

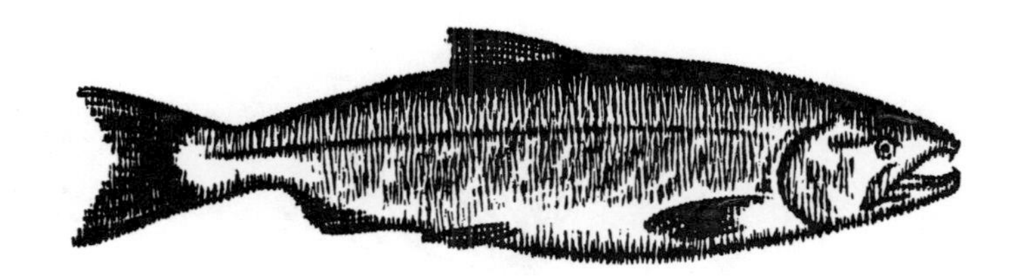

DANISH SANDWICHES

1 - 7½ oz. can salmon, drained
2 tablespoons celery, chopped
2 tablespoons green onion, finely chopped
2 tablespoons mayonnaise
2 teaspoons lemon juice
dash pepper
¼ teaspoon dried dill weed
6 slices whole wheat bread
bibb lettuce
cucumber, thinly sliced
radish, thinly sliced
parsley sprigs

Flake salmon. Combine salmon, celery, green onion, mayonnaise, lemon juice, pepper and dill weed. Place a leaf of lettuce on each slice of bread. Overlap cucumber and radish slices on each sandwich. Mound salmon mixture in center. Garnish with parsley sprigs. Makes 6 servings.

155 calories per serving *7.5 grams fat per serving*
345 mg sodium per serving *20 mg cholesterol per serving*

Substitutions: *canned water-packed tuna, any cooked, flaked fish, cooked shrimp meat*

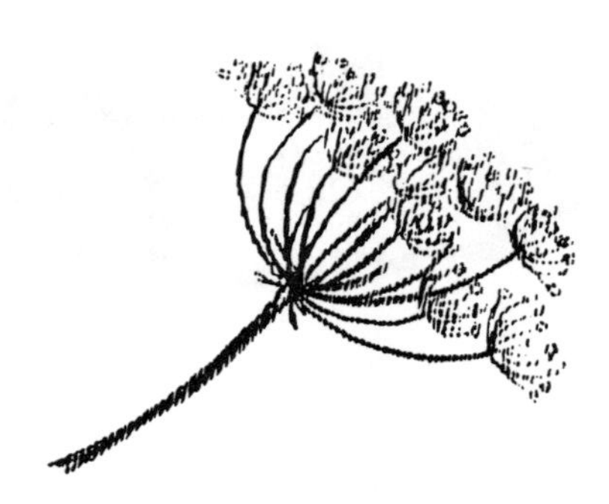

SALMON IN PITA BREAD

1 - 7½ oz. can salmon, drained
¼ cup garbanzo beans, coarsely chopped
¼ cup celery, chopped
2 tablespoons onion, chopped
1 tablespoon fresh parsley, chopped
¼ cup plain low fat yogurt
dash pepper
dash dried oregano
lettuce, shredded
2 pita bread, halved
1 tomato, cut into wedges

Drain salmon and flake. Combine with beans, celery, onion and parsley. Combine yogurt, pepper and oregano; gently toss with salmon mixture. Place lettuce in pita bread halves, distribute salmon mixture evenly over lettuce. Garnish with tomato wedges. Makes 4 servings.

200 calories per serving *6 grams fat per serving*
435 mg sodium per serving *30 mg cholesterol per serving*

Substitutions: *canned water-packed tuna, imitation crab*

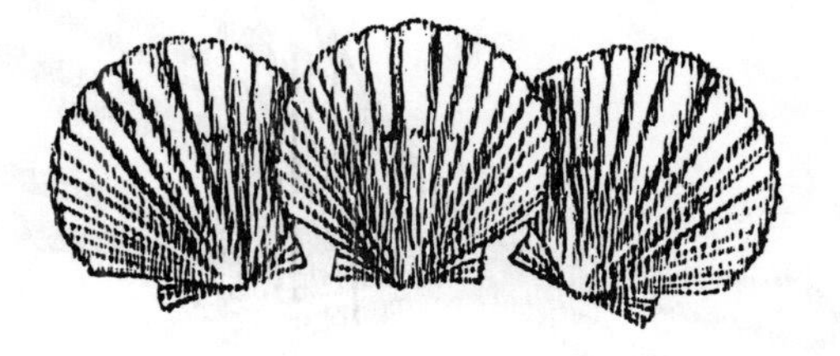

CHAPTER FIVE

ENTREES: FISH

CHAPTER 5

ENTREES: FISH

ORIENTAL STIR-FRY

1 lb. albacore tuna

Marinade:
½ cup white wine
1 teaspoon fresh ginger, grated
2 cloves garlic, minced
½ teaspoon onion powder
½ teaspoon pepper
2 teaspoons sugar
1 tablespoon sesame oil

1 tablespoon margarine
2 cups mushrooms, sliced
½ cup celery, sliced on the diagonal
½ cup green onion, chopped
1 cup broccoli, sliced on the diagonal

Cut fish into 1-inch cubes. To make marinade: combine wine, ginger, garlic, onion powder, pepper, sugar and sesame oil. Marinate fish for 15 minutes. Melt margarine in a wok or frying pan. Add vegetables and cook until tender-crisp. Add fish with marinade to vegetables and cook at medium heat until fish flakes when tested with a fork. Serve with brown rice and fresh fruit plate. Makes 4 servings.

200 calories per serving — *8 grams fat per serving*
145 mg sodium per serving — *50 mg cholesterol per serving*

Substitutions: *halibut, swordfish, marlin*

Don't be put off when you first see albacore tuna. The meat will be somewhat pinkish colored and a little soft. It will be lovely, white firm fillets when it is cooked.

OVEN-POACHED ALBACORE TUNA

1 lb. albacore tuna
1 quart water
½ cup white vinegar
1 bay leaf
1 medium onion, sliced
1 carrot, diced
½ teaspoon salt (optional)

Arrange albacore in a 9x13-inch baking pan at least 2 inches deep. In a saucepan combine water, vinegar, bay leaf, onion, carrots and salt. Heat to simmering and pour over fish. Cover pan tightly with foil and bake at 400° for about 20 minutes or until fish flakes when tested with a fork. Remove from oven and carefully lift the albacore from the poaching liquid. Serve hot or chill. Poached albacore makes a fine entrée or may be substituted in any recipe requiring canned tuna. Makes 4 servings.

140 calories per serving | *3.5 grams fat per serving*
325 mg sodium per serving | *60 mg cholesterol per serving*

Substitutions: *salmon, bluefish, red snapper*

Albacore is a premium tuna. The color of its flesh ranges from light beige to pink. The flesh turns white when cooked. Its texture is firm and flavor is mild. Albacore tuna can be baked, poached, microwaved, sautéed, broiled or grilled.

PARMESAN CATFISH

½ cup Parmesan cheese, grated
¼ cup flour
½ teaspoon pepper
1 teaspoon paprika
2 lbs. catfish fillets, skinless and boneless
2 tablespoons margarine, melted

Combine Parmesan cheese, flour and seasonings in a bag. Place catfish in bag and shake to coat with cheese mixture. Place in baking dish. Pour remaining cheese mixture onto fish. Pour margarine over catfish and bake at 400° until golden brown and fish flakes when tested with a fork, approximately 15-20 minutes. Serve with corn bread and melon. Makes 8 servings.

190 calories per serving | *8 grams fat per serving*
200 mg sodium per serving | *80 mg cholesterol per serving*

Substitutions: *rockfish (snapper), pollock, hoki*

The Channel catfish is the main commercial species of the many freshwater catfish species. About 80% of the domestic catfish harvest is from Mississippi where catfish is raised in 70,000-acre ponds. Fresh farm-raised catfish is available year-round, but the peak harvesting season is from late summer to late fall. Catfish is excellent baked, broiled, stuffed, barbecued, sautéed and steamed.

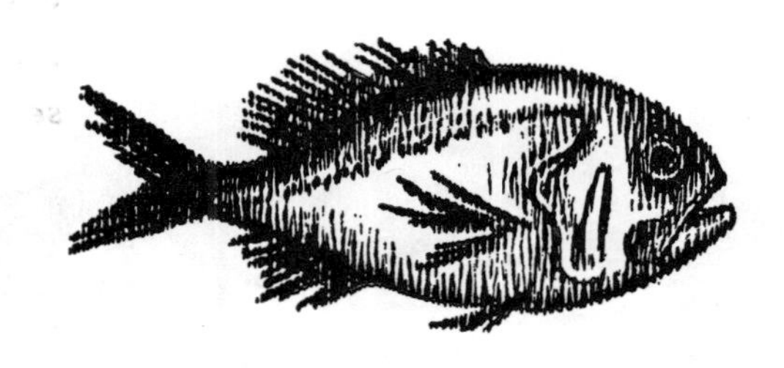

CATFISH ETTOUFFÉE

1 lb. catfish, cut in large pieces
¼ teaspoon pepper
dash cayenne pepper
2 teaspoons vegetable oil
2 cloves garlic, minced
1 tablespoon fresh parsley, chopped
¼ large bell pepper, chopped
1 stalk celery, chopped
¼ cup green onion, chopped
1 tablespoon flour
1 - 8 oz. can tomato sauce
½ teaspoon dried thyme
1 bay leaf
1 slice lemon
1 tablespoon water

Select a black iron pot or saucepan that you can handle well enough to shake, as you never stir the fish while it is cooking. Rub the pieces of fish well with a mixture of black and red pepper. Put oil in the unheated pot. Arrange half of the fish on the bottom. Mix the chopped vegetables and sprinkle half over fish. Sprinkle half of flour over the vegetables and half of the tomato sauce and then repeat layers. Add the thyme, bay leaf, lemon and water. Place pot over low heat and cook slowly for one hour or until fish flakes when tested with a fork. Shake pot often to keep from sticking. Never stir as this will break the fish. When tender, taste for seasoning and add more if necessary. Serve over rice. Makes 4 servings.

160 calories per serving *5 grams fat per serving*
400 mg sodium per serving *60 mg cholesterol per serving*

Substitutions: *tilapia, ocean perch, cod*

POACHED COD WITH HERBS

1 lb. cod fillets
4 cups water
2 tablespoons margarine
½ cup each onion, carrots and celery, chopped
2 cloves garlic, minced
6 peppercorns
3-4 whole allspice
1 teaspoon bouquet garni or fine herbs (can be made by combining equal portions of the following: dried dill weed, thyme, basil, parsley, marjoram and tarragon)
2 tablespoons lemon juice

CONVENTIONAL METHOD:
Combine ingredients, except fish, in a skillet or 3-quart saucepan and bring to a boil. Reduce heat, cover and simmer 15-20 minutes. Place fish fillets in simmering liquid and cover until done. Remove fish with large spatula. Poached fish may be served with a squeeze of lemon or Skinny-Dip Tartar Sauce (see page 236), boiled potatoes and fresh vegetables. It may also be served cold. Makes 4 servings.

MICROWAVE METHOD:
In 2-quart glass casserole, combine all ingredients except fish. Bring liquid to a full boil at full power; cook additional 5 minutes. Gently place fish in poaching liquid. Cover with wax paper. Cook at medium power. Allow 7-10 minutes for thick fillets and 3-5 minutes for thinner fillets. Do not overcook! It may be necessary to turn the thick fillets once and rearrange in dish.

160 calories per serving *7.8 grams fat per serving*
175 mg sodium per serving *60 mg cholesterol per serving*

Substitutions: *sea bass, salmon, orange roughy*

BASIL BAKED COD

1 lb. cod
1 tablespoon margarine
1 tablespoon lemon juice
¼ teaspoon onion powder
½ teaspoon dried basil
½ red bell pepper, thinly sliced

Place fish in baking dish. Melt margarine; add lemon juice and pour over fish. Sprinkle onion powder and basil over fish. Garnish with bell pepper slices. Cover and bake at 400° for 10-15 minutes or until fish flakes when tested with a fork. Serve with baked potatoes topped with plain low fat yogurt and steamed fresh vegetables. Makes 4 servings.

115 calories per serving *4.4 grams fat per serving*
115 mg sodium per serving *60 mg cholesterol per serving*

Substitutions: *salmon, halibut, catfish*

CROAKER STIR-FRY

1½ lbs. croaker fillets, skinless and boneless

Marinade:
3 tablespoons lemon juice
2 tablespoons light soy sauce

2 tablespoons vegetable oil, divided
1 cup carrots, thinly sliced
1 cup broccoli, thinly sliced
1 cup mushrooms, sliced
¾ cup green onion, cut into ½-inch lengths
2 medium tomatoes, cut into eighths
2½ tablespoons cornstarch
¼ teaspoon pepper
1 cup cold water
reserved marinade

Cut fish into ¾-inch strips and place in bowl. Combine lemon juice and soy sauce and pour over fish. Marinate while preparing vegetables. After vegetables are ready, heat 1 tablespoon oil in wok or skillet. Add carrots and stir-fry for 2 minutes. Add remaining vegetables and stir-fry for another 2 minutes. Remove vegetables to a warm platter. Add remaining 1 tablespoon oil to wok. Drain fish strips; reserve marinade. Stir-fry fish strips for approximately 2 minutes or until fish is opaque and flakes when tested with a fork. Add vegetables to fish in wok. Combine cornstarch, pepper, cold water and reserved marinade; mix well. Add to fish mixture and stir only until broth is clear and thickened. Serve over rice. Makes 6 servings.

190 calories per serving *5.7 grams fat per serving*
375 mg sodium per serving *55 mg cholesterol per serving*

Substitutions: *squid strips, halibut, scallops*

CRISPY BAKED FLOUNDER

1 lb. flounder fillets
dash pepper
2 tablespoons vegetable oil
⅓ cup seasoned bread crumbs

Season fillets with pepper, dip in oil and coat with bread crumbs. Arrange in a single layer in a lightly-oiled shallow baking dish. Bake 10 minutes at 500° without turning or basting. Serve with green beans and boiled new potatoes, cut in quarters. Makes 4 servings.

145 calories per serving *7.5 grams fat per serving*
85 mg sodium per serving *50 mg cholesterol per serving*

Substitutions: *sole, tilapia, hoki*

This recipe is a tasty, light alternative to deep-fat frying.

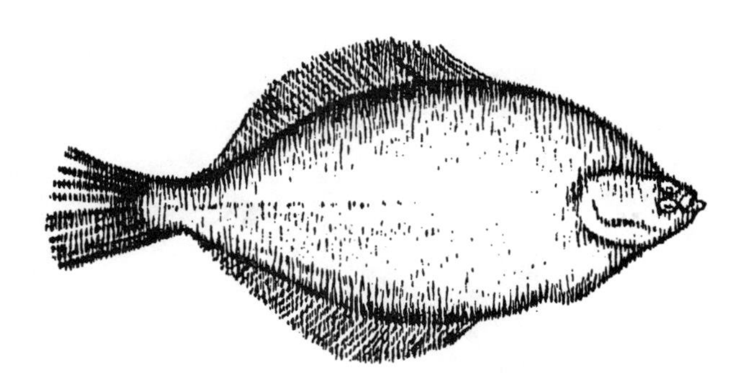

ITALIAN FLOUNDER ROLL-UPS

1 lb. flounder
1 - 10 oz. package frozen french-style green beans
2 tablespoons onion, chopped
1 - 8 oz. can tomato sauce
¼ teaspoon dried oregano
¼ teaspoon dried basil
⅛ teaspoon garlic powder
2 tablespoons Parmesan cheese, grated

Divide fish into 4 servings. Set aside. Add green beans and onion to boiling water. Cover and simmer gently until beans are tender-crisp, about 7 minutes. Drain. Place ¼ of the green bean-onion mixture in middle of each fish portion. Start with narrow end of fillet and roll. Place in baking pan with the end of fillets underneath. Mix tomato sauce, oregano, basil and garlic powder. Pour over fish roll-ups. Sprinkle with cheese. Bake at 400° until fish flakes when tested with a fork, about 15-20 minutes. Serve with yellow summer squash and bran muffins. Makes 4 servings.

125 calories per serving *1.5 grams fat per serving*
400 mg sodium per serving *50 mg cholesterol per serving*

Substitutions: *cod, sole, hoki*

FIVE-SPICE HADDOCK

1 teaspoon ground cinnamon
¼ teaspoon ground nutmeg
½ teaspoon garlic powder
½ teaspoon paprika
¼ teaspoon coarse ground pepper
2 tablespoons vegetable oil
1½ lbs. haddock fillets
1 tablespoon fresh parsley, chopped

Combine spices in flat dish. Spread oil over fillets and roll in spice mixture until coated evenly. Transfer fillets to baking dish. Bake at 450° until fish flakes when tested with a fork. Garnish with parsley. Makes 6 servings.

120 calories per serving *5.5 grams fat per serving*
70 mg sodium per serving *80 mg cholesterol per serving*

Substitutions: *orange roughy, cod, rockfish (snapper), Northern pike*

OLD-FASHIONED STUFFED HADDOCK

2 lbs. haddock fillets

Stuffing:
2 teaspoons vegetable oil
¼ cup onion, chopped
¼ cup celery, chopped
2 cups bread cubes, soft
4 teaspoons parsley, chopped, divided
¼ teaspoon dried sage
⅛ teaspoon pepper
1 tablespoon margarine, melted
¼ cup low sodium chicken broth

Lightly oil shallow baking pan. Heat 2 teaspoons oil in small frypan. Add onion and celery. Cover and cook, stirring occasionally, until vegetables are tender. Stir in bread cubes, 3 teaspoons of parsley, sage and pepper. Pour chicken broth over stuffing and toss. Arrange half of fillets in baking pan. Spread bread mixture over fillets in pan. Top with remaining fillets. Cover and bake at 400° for 15-20 minutes. Mix margarine with remaining parsley. Spoon over fish fillets. Continue baking, uncovered, until fish flakes when tested with a fork, about 5 minutes. Serve with sliced tomatoes and salad greens. Makes 8 servings.

150 calories per serving *2.5 grams fat per serving*
160 mg sodium per serving *70 mg cholesterol per serving*

Substitutions: *whole dressed trout, salmon or mackerel*

ORIENTAL HALIBUT SAUTÉ

1 clove garlic, minced
2 tablespoons margarine
2 cups mushrooms, sliced
1 lb. halibut, skinless, cut into 1-inch cubes
½ cup white wine
2 tablespoons light soy sauce
¼ cup green onion, sliced

Sauté garlic in melted margarine. Add mushrooms; sauté and stir 1 minute. Add halibut to mushroom mixture and sauté 2-3 minutes. Add wine and soy sauce and bring to a boil. Reduce heat and simmer until fish flakes when tested with a fork. Sprinkle with green onion and serve over rice. Makes 4 servings.

215 calories per serving *6.9 grams fat per serving*
545 mg sodium per serving *55 mg cholesterol per serving*

***Substitutions:** albacore tuna, ahi (yellowfin tuna), marlin*

OVEN-FRIED HALIBUT

2 tablespoons margarine
1 tablespoon lemon juice
½ cup dry bread crumbs
½ teaspoon paprika
½ teaspoon pepper
½ teaspoon garlic powder
1½ lbs. halibut steaks or fillets

Melt margarine in saucepan; add lemon juice. Set aside. Combine bread crumbs, paprika, pepper and garlic powder in a bowl. Dip halibut into melted margarine and lemon juice, then into crumb mixture, coating all sides. Place in single layer in lightly-oiled baking dish. Bake at 450° about 10-20 minutes or until halibut flakes when tested with a fork. Serve with boiled potatoes and steamed vegetables. Makes 6 servings.

180 calories per serving *5.3 grams fat per serving*
170 mg sodium per serving *5 mg cholesterol per serving*

Substitutions: *cod, rockfish (snapper), sea bass*

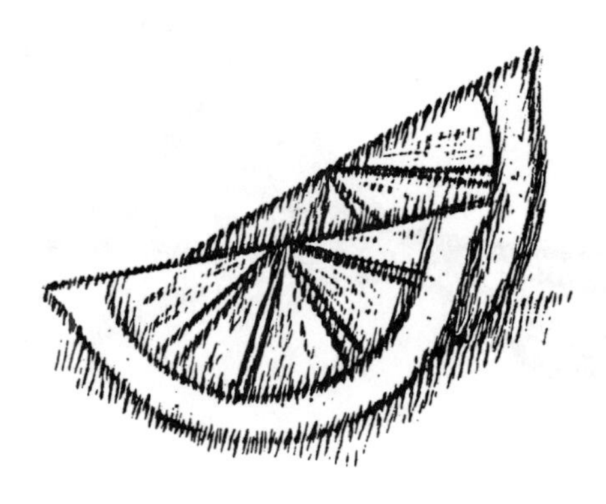

GRILLED HALIBUT MEXICANA

1 lb. halibut steaks or fillets

Marinade:
⅓ cup lime juice
3 cloves garlic, minced
1 tablespoon vegetable oil
¼ cup beer
1 tablespoon fresh parsley, chopped
½ teaspoon cumin
2 teaspoons Dijon mustard
pepper to taste

Salsa *(see page 248)*

Place halibut in marinade dish and set aside. Combine remaining ingredients except Salsa; pour over halibut. Cover and marinate in refrigerator for 1 hour, turning once. While halibut is marinating, make Salsa. Drain halibut reserving marinade. Place on lightly-oiled grill, 4-5 inches over hot charcoals. Cook 4-5 minutes; baste with marinade and turn. Cook an additional 4-5 minutes or until halibut flakes when tested with a fork. Top with Salsa. Makes 4 servings.

165 calories per serving *5 grams fat per serving*
100 mg sodium per serving *55 mg cholesterol per serving*

Substitutions: *orange roughy, cod, hoki*

HOKI SAUTÉ

1 lb. hoki fillets
2 tablespoons vegetable oil
1 cup carrots, thinly sliced
1 cup celery, sliced
1 cup green onion, chopped
1 cup broccoli, chopped
½ teaspoon fresh ginger, grated, or
¼ teaspoon ground ginger
¼ cup white wine
2 teaspoons cornstarch
1 teaspoon lemon peel, grated
pepper
red bell pepper, cut in strips

Cut hoki into 1-inch cubes. Set aside. Heat oil in skillet and sauté vegetables until tender-crisp. Add fish to skillet and sauté until fish just begins to turn opaque. Add ginger. Combine wine, cornstarch and lemon peel; add to fish mixture. Cook and stir until thickened and fish flakes when tested with a fork. Season to taste with pepper. Garnish with red pepper. Serve with rice. Makes 4 servings.

225 calories per serving *9 grams fat per serving*
100 mg sodium per serving *45 mg cholesterol per serving*

Substitutions: *sole, flounder, peeled and deveined shrimp (prawns)*

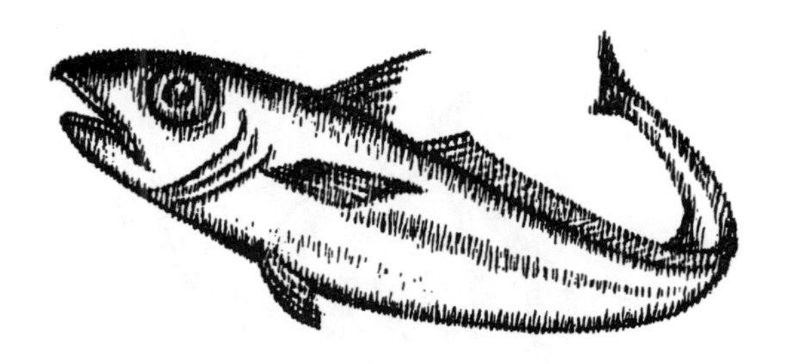

EVERYBODY'S MACKEREL

½ cup fresh parsley, chopped
1 teaspoon dried dill weed
¼ cup fresh chives, chopped
¼ cup onion, chopped
2 tablespoons lemon juice
2 lbs. whole dressed mackerel

Mix together parsley, dill weed, chives, onion and lemon juice and sprinkle inside fish. Wrap fish in aluminum foil, sealing the edges carefully. Bake at 400° for 20-30 minutes or until fish flakes when tested with a fork. Unwrap and remove to a hot platter; garnish with parsley and lemon slices. Makes 8 servings.

160 calories per serving | *7.3 grams fat per serving*
80 mg sodium per serving | *40 mg cholesterol per serving*

Substitutions: *whole dressed trout, salmon or bluefish*

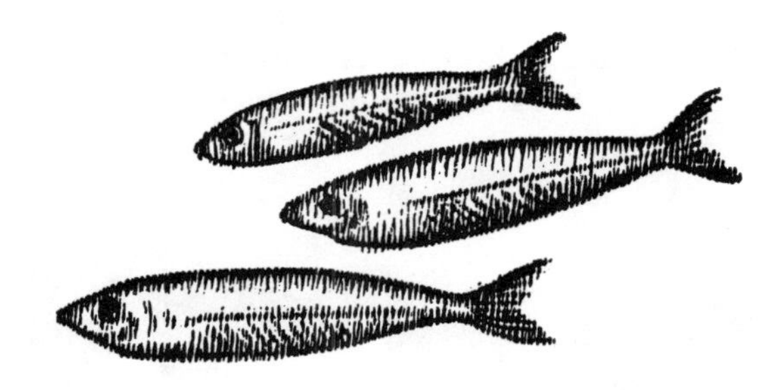

MACADAMIA BAKED MAHI MAHI

¼ cup flour
¼ teaspoon onion powder
⅛ teaspoon pepper
1 tablespoon margarine
1 lb. mahi mahi
6 macadamia nuts, chopped

Combine flour and seasonings. Melt margarine in shallow baking dish in oven. Dredge mahi mahi in flour mixture; place in dish. Turn mahi mahi to coat with margarine; place in baking dish and sprinkle with macadamia nuts. Bake at 400° for 10 minutes or until mahi mahi flakes when tested with a fork. Serve with fresh pineapple slices and sweet potatoes. Makes 4 servings.

215 calories per serving | *8.0 grams fat per serving*
155 mg sodium per serving | *90 mg cholesterol per serving*

Substitutions: *lingcod, sturgeon, whitefish*

Mahi mahi is the popular Hawaiian name for the dolphinfish, which is not related to the marine mammal called the dolphin. Found in tropical and subtropical waters throughout the world, dolphinfish inhabit the warmer waters of both the Atlantic and Pacific coasts. The white flesh is firm with solid flakes and delicate flavor. Mahi mahi is considered by many to be one of the most delicious seafoods.

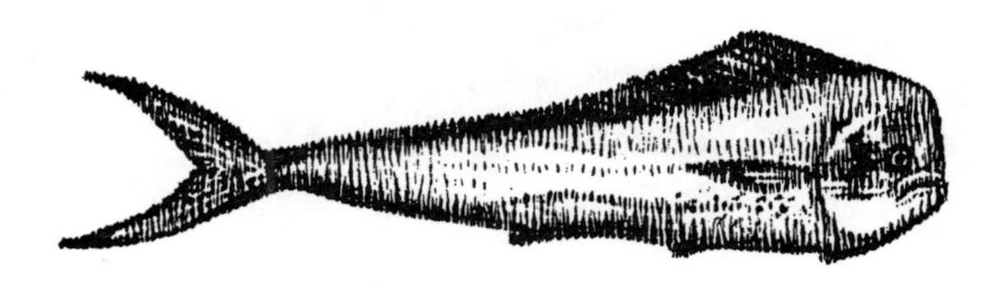

MONKFISH WITH ORIENTAL SAUCE

"A Family Favorite"

Sauce:
¼ cup orange juice
2 tablespoons vegetable oil
2 tablespoons light soy sauce
1 tablespoon lemon juice
1 clove garlic, minced
⅛ teaspoon pepper

2 lbs. monkfish fillets

Combine sauce ingredients. Brush all sides of fish with sauce. Place fish on lightly-oiled grill over hot charcoals. Also excellent when broiled. Brush fish frequently with sauce during cooking. Serve with baked potatoes and steamed carrots. Makes 8 servings.

120 calories per serving | *4.7 grams fat per serving*
218 mg sodium per serving | *40 mg cholesterol per serving*

Substitutions: *halibut, halibut cheeks*

LEMON BROILED OCEAN PERCH

Marinade:
juice of 1 lemon
grated peel of 1 lemon
1 tablespoon brown sugar
1 tablespoon vegetable oil

1 lb. ocean perch fillets
lemon wedges
parsley

To make marinade: in a baking dish combine lemon juice, lemon peel, brown sugar and oil. Mix well. Place fish in a single layer in marinade, turn to coat both sides. Cover and marinate in refrigerator for 1 hour, turning once. Lightly oil broiler pan. Transfer fish to broiler pan, reserving marinade. Baste fish with marinade during broiling. Broil 4-5 inches from heat source for 5-7 minutes or until fish flakes when tested with a fork. Garnish with lemon wedges and parsley. Serve with rice and steamed carrots. Makes 4 servings.

130 calories per serving | *4.5 grams fat per serving*
70 mg sodium per serving | *60 mg cholesterol per serving*

Substitutions: *rockfish (snapper), catfish, sablefish (black cod)*

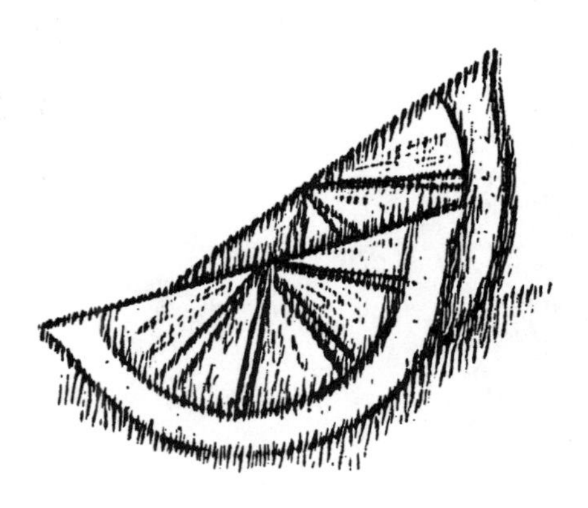

ORANGE ROUGHY UNDER ORANGE SAUCE

2 lbs. orange roughy fillets
1 tablespoon margarine
1 teaspoon flour
½ cup orange juice
2 teaspoons lemon juice
dash nutmeg
¼ teaspoon salt (optional)

Cut orange roughy into 8 portions. Set aside. Melt margarine in a pan and add flour, stirring well until blended. Mix in remaining ingredients, stirring over low heat until thickened. Broil orange roughy 4 inches from heat source until fish flakes when tested with a fork. Pour orange sauce over the fish and serve immediately. Makes 8 servings.

95 calories per serving 1.7 grams fat per serving
85 mg sodium per serving (calculated without salt)
66 mg cholesterol per serving

Substitutions: *cod, albacore tuna, catfish*

SPICY GRILLED ORANGE ROUGHY

Sauce:
½ cup tomato sauce
2 tablespoons green onion, minced
1 tablespoon parsley, minced
½ teaspoon Worcestershire sauce
⅛ teaspoon pepper
⅛ teaspoon fresh basil leaves, crushed
dash sugar

1 tablespoon vegetable oil
2 teaspoons lemon juice
2 lbs. orange roughy

To make sauce: combine tomato sauce, green onion, parsley, Worcestershire sauce, pepper, basil and sugar in saucepan. Cook and stir 5 minutes over medium heat. Set aside. Mix oil and lemon juice; brush on both sides of the fish. Grill orange roughy 4 inches from hot charcoals for 5 minutes. Turn fish, baste with tomato mixture and continue cooking until orange roughy flakes when tested with a fork. Thoroughly heat remaining sauce; serve over orange roughy. This recipe may be broiled in oven. Serve with hot French bread and sliced tomatoes and cucumber. Makes 8 servings.

95 calories per serving *2 grams fat per serving*
180 mg sodium per serving *66 mg cholesterol per serving*

Substitutions: *sablefish (black cod), haddock, salmon*

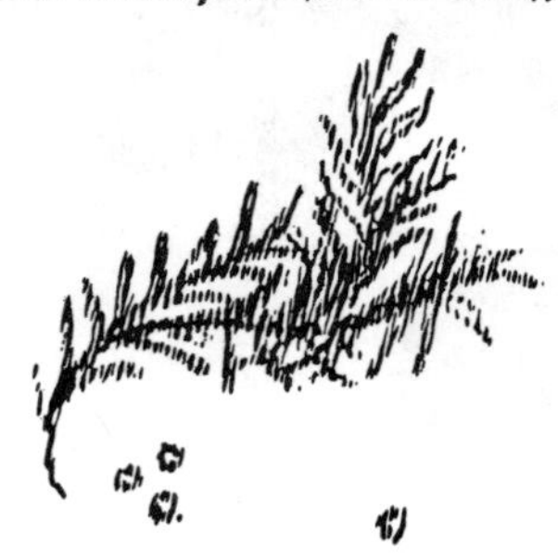

HURRY UP BAKED POLLOCK

"A Meal In Twenty-Minutes"

1 lb. pollock fillets
1 tablespoon margarine, melted
⅓ cup dry bread crumbs
¼ teaspoon onion powder
½ teaspoon dried basil
1 tablespoon lemon juice

Brush fillets with melted margarine to coat all sides. Combine bread crumbs, onion powder and basil and dredge fillets. Place coated fillets in an 8x8-inch baking dish. Sprinkle lemon juice over fish. Bake at 400° for 10-15 minutes or until fish flakes when tested with a fork. Serve with rice and steamed vegetables for a meal in 20 minutes. Makes 4 servings.

140 calories per serving *3.8 grams fat per serving*
150 mg sodium per serving *50 mg cholesterol per serving*

Substitutions: *catfish, cod, halibut*

Pollock is one of the most plentiful resources in the North Pacific's fishing industry. It is a very lean fish with a fairly firm texture and a delicate flavor. It is marketed in 3 to 10-ounce waste-free fillets.

MEXICAN-STYLE ROCKFISH

¼ cup green onion, chopped
1 tablespoon margarine
2 medium tomatoes, chopped
3 tablespoons fresh lime juice
1 oz. canned green chiles, diced
1 tablespoon fresh parsley, minced
⅛ teaspoon salt
⅛ teaspoon garlic powder
pepper to taste
1 lb. rockfish (snapper)
lime wedges

Sauté onion in margarine until tender. Add remaining ingredients except fish and lime wedges. Bring to a boil; reduce heat and simmer 10 minutes. Place snapper in skillet; spoon sauce over fish. Cover and simmer 10 minutes or until fish flakes when tested with a fork. Serve with Spanish rice and papaya. Garnish with lime wedges. Makes 4 servings.

130 calories per serving *4.4 grams fat per serving*
185 mg sodium per serving *60 mg cholesterol per serving*

Substitutions: *red snapper, orange roughy, pollock*

LEMON BAKED ROCKFISH

½ cup onion, chopped, divided in half
¾ cup fresh tomato, chopped
½ cup celery, finely chopped
1 lb. rockfish (snapper)
4 teaspoons Worcestershire sauce
1 tablespoon lemon juice
¼ cup parsley, chopped
lemon wedges for garnish

Combine ¼ cup of the onion with the tomato and celery. Sprinkle over bottom of an 8x8-inch baking pan. Place fish fillets over vegetables. Mix Worcestershire sauce and lemon juice; spoon over fish. Sprinkle with remaining ¼ cup onion. Bake at 400° for 10-15 minutes or until fish flakes when tested with a fork. Sprinkle with parsley. Garnish with lemon wedges. Serve with green salad and whole wheat roll. Makes 4 servings.

130 calories per serving *2 grams fat per serving*
120 mg sodium per serving *45 mg cholesterol per serving*

Substitutions: *orange roughy, salmon, haddock*

Rockfish (snapper) and red snapper are technically different species of fish. However, either may be used in our recipes.

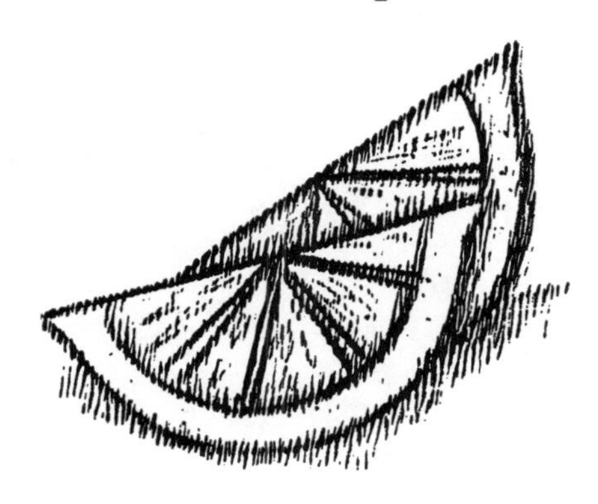

OVEN-POACHED ROCKFISH

4 cups skim milk
1 tablespoon margarine
dash of white pepper
¼ cup green onion, chopped
1½ lbs. rockfish (snapper)

Preheat oven to 400°. Mix skim milk, margarine, white pepper and green onion in 8x8-inch baking pan. Cover and heat to simmering in the oven. Add rockfish and cook until fish flakes when tested with a fork, approximately 10 minutes. Makes 4 servings.

277 calories per serving
6.5 grams fat per serving
275 mg sodium per serving
65 mg cholesterol per serving

Substitutions: *halibut, grouper, cod*

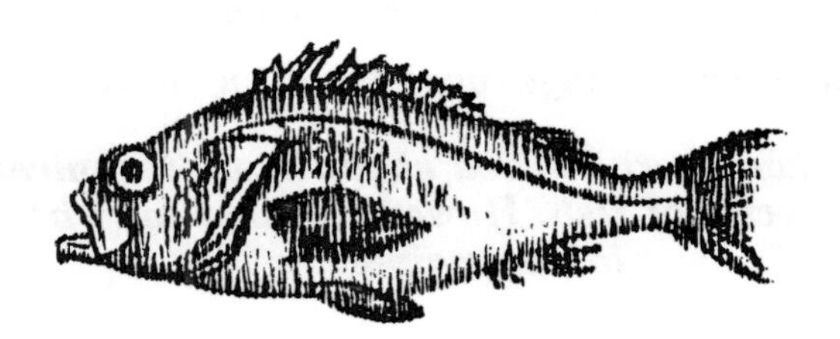

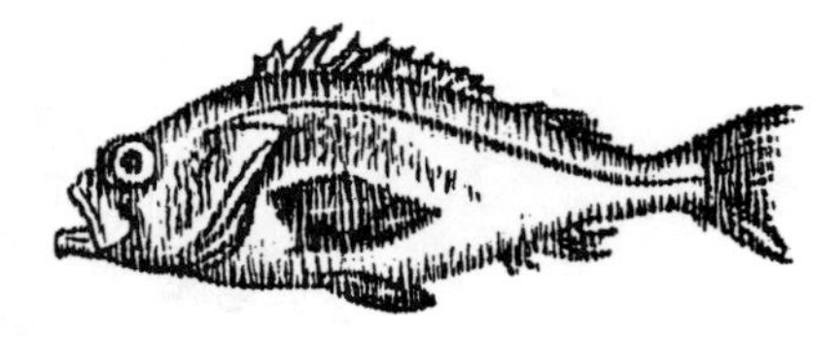

ROCKFISH WITH LEMON-TARRAGON SAUCE

1 lb. rockfish (snapper) fillets
1 quart water
¼ cup lemon juice
1 small onion, sliced
1 bay leaf
4 peppercorns
4 whole cloves

Lemon-Tarragon Sauce:
2 tablespoons margarine
1 tablespoon lemon juice
½ teaspoon dried tarragon
¼ teaspoon salt (optional)
parsley, chopped

Cut rockfish into 1-inch cubes. In a saucepan combine water, lemon juice, onion and seasonings. Bring to boil; simmer 20 minutes. Add rockfish. Simmer, covered, 5-10 minutes until rockfish flakes when tested with a fork. While rockfish is simmering prepare Lemon-Tarragon Sauce. In a small saucepan, melt margarine and add lemon juice, tarragon and salt. Remove rockfish from water and serve on a platter with Lemon-Tarragon Sauce poured over it; garnish with parsley. Serve with boiled new potatoes and peas. Makes 4 servings.

135 calories per serving 6.5 grams fat per serving
150 mg sodium per serving (calculated without salt)
45 mg cholesterol per serving

Substitutions: *cod, halibut, salmon*

BAYSIDE ROCKFISH

1 lb. rockfish (snapper) fillets, cut into 4 portions
2 tablespoons margarine
2 tablespoons lemon juice
¼ teaspoon pepper
½ cup carrots, finely chopped
¼ cup celery, finely chopped
¼ cup green onion, chopped
1 tablespoon fresh parsley, chopped
½ lemon, thinly sliced

Place each fish fillet on a piece of foil about 4 inches longer than the rockfish. Melt margarine and add lemon juice, pepper, carrots, celery, onion and parsley. Pour mixture over rockfish fillets. Top with lemon slices. Bring edges of foil together and fold over several times. To form fish-shaped foil package, twist one end to form a tail. Tuck the other end under to form a point, or nose of the fish. Place on cooking sheet and bake at 400° for 15-20 minutes or until fish flakes when tested with a fork. Makes 4 servings.

170 calories per serving — *7.3 grams fat per serving*
140 mg sodium per serving — *45 mg cholesterol per serving*

Substitutions: *cod, pollock, halibut*

Pre-package and take along for an open-pit beach barbecue.

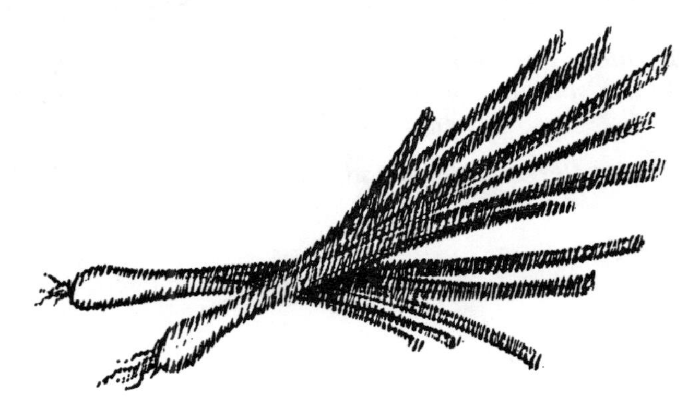

SESAME SABLEFISH (BLACK COD)

1 lb. sablefish (black cod) fillets

Marinade:
¼ cup orange juice
2 tablespoons catsup
2 tablespoons light soy sauce
1 tablespoon lemon juice
¼ teaspoon pepper
1 teaspoon sesame oil
1 tablespoon brown sugar

Cut fish into 4 portions. Place fish in a single layer in baking dish. To make marinade: in small bowl combine orange juice, catsup, soy sauce, lemon juice, pepper, sesame oil and brown sugar. Pour over fish. Cover and marinate in refrigerator for 30 minutes, turning once. Remove fish, reserving marinade. Coat broiler pan lightly with vegetable oil; place fish on broiler pan; baste with marinade. Broil 4-5 inches from heat source for 5-7 minutes. Turn and baste with marinade. Broil for an additional 4-5 minutes or until fish flakes when tested with a fork. Heat remaining marinade and pour over fish. Serve with rice and pineapple slices. Makes 4 servings.

190 calories per serving *7.6 grams fat per serving*
545 mg sodium per serving *65 mg cholesterol per serving*

Substitutions: *trout fillets, swordfish, shark*

Sablefish/black cod is caught from California to Alaska by a variety of methods including longlining, potfishing and trawling. Because of its high (15-20%) oil content, sablefish has an excellent flavor and is adaptable to a number of cooking methods. A Scandinavian favorite is boiled black cod and potatoes.

BARBECUED SALMON

1 lb. salmon steaks or fillets
Snappy Barbecue Sauce (see page 238)
or
Barbecue Basting Sauce (see page 239)

Place salmon steaks or fillets in a tray made of heavy duty foil with 1-inch sides. Place on grill over hot charcoals. Cook for 5-20 minutes until fish flakes when tested with a fork. The fish may be basted during the last 2-3 minutes of cooking with about ½ cup Snappy Barbecue Sauce or Barbecue Basting Sauce. Basting will keep the fish moist. Serve with salad, whole grain rolls, fresh vegetables and fruit. Hint: For extra moist fish, place foil lightly over top of seafood during cooking. Makes 4 servings.

160 calories per serving *7.7 grams fat per serving*
60 mg sodium per serving *70 mg cholesterol per serving*

Substitutions: *swordfish, halibut, shark*

Kick off your Fourth of July picnic with barbecued salmon. Salmon supplies are plentiful during summer and fall.

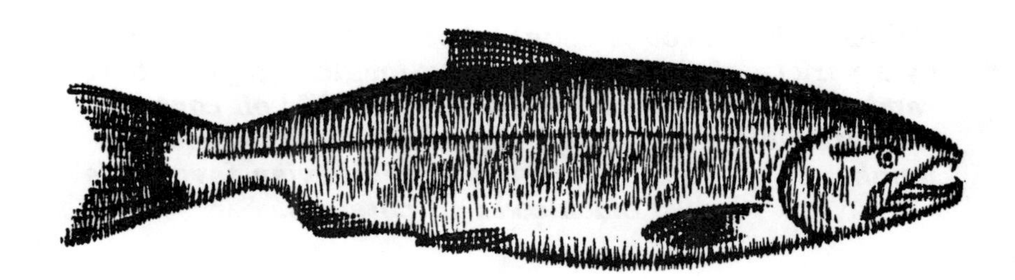

SIMPLY BAKED SALMON

3 lbs. whole dressed salmon
pepper
1 teaspoon garlic powder
1 teaspoon dried dill weed
1 tablespoon margarine
lemon juice
1 onion, thinly sliced
1 cup celery, finely chopped

Rinse salmon. Cut head and tail off, if desired. Sprinkle pepper, garlic powder and dill weed inside and outside of salmon. Put dabs of margarine and squeeze lemon juice inside salmon cavity. Place onion and celery inside the salmon. Wrap in foil. Bake at 400° for 30 minutes. Cook until fish flakes when tested with a fork. Serve with boiled potatoes and green salad. Makes 8 servings.

175 calories per serving *9 grams fat per serving*
75 mg sodium per serving *75 mg cholesterol per serving*

Substitutions: *whole dressed trout or mackerel*

This method of baking can be used with any variety and size of dressed fish.

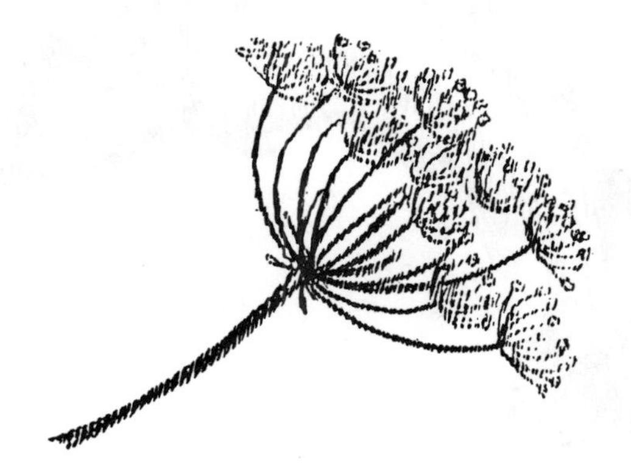

BROILED SALMON STEAKS WITH HERB SAUCE

1 lb. salmon steaks
1 tablespoon margarine
¼ cup dry white wine
1 tablespoon fresh parsley, chopped
¼ teaspoon fine herbs or bouquet garni
1 clove garlic, minced

Combine margarine, wine, parsley, herbs and garlic in a saucepan; heat slowly until margarine is melted. Let stand 15 minutes. Place fish on broiler pan; brush fish with sauce. Broil about 4 inches from heat source, 4-6 minutes. Turn carefully; brush with sauce. Broil 4-6 minutes longer or until fish flakes when tested with a fork. Can be barbecued instead of broiled. Serve with baked potatoes and baked squash. Makes 4 servings.

190 calories per serving *10 grams fat per serving*
90 mg sodium per serving *75 mg cholesterol per serving*

***Substitutions:** trout fillets, sablefish (black cod), bluefish*

SCANDINAVIAN SALMON STEAKS WITH SPINACH

1 lb. salmon steaks
pepper
1 teaspoon dried dill weed
1 tablespoon margarine
1 large onion, chopped
1 clove garlic, minced
2 lbs. fresh spinach, washed, with leaves cut into 1-inch wide strips
lemon slices

Arrange salmon on a lightly-oiled broiler pan; broil 4 inches from the heat source for 5 minutes. Turn steaks and season with pepper. Sprinkle with dill weed. Broil steaks for about 5 minutes more or until fish flakes when tested with a fork. Meanwhile, in a large frying pan, melt margarine and sauté the onion and garlic until tender. Stir in the spinach (with the water that clings to the leaves). Cover pan and cook over high heat for about 3 minutes. Stir occasionally. To serve, spoon spinach onto a rimmed serving platter. Lay salmon steaks and lemon slices on top. Serve with boiled new potatoes. Makes 4 servings.

225 calories per serving *11 grams fat per serving*
250 mg sodium per serving *75 mg cholesterol per serving*

***Substitutions:** trout fillets, bluefish*

SALMON TERIYAKI

Marinade:
3 tablespoons light soy sauce
¼ cup white wine
½ cup brown sugar
½ teaspoon ground ginger or
1 teaspoon fresh ginger, grated

1 lb. salmon steaks or fillets

To make marinade: combine soy sauce, wine, brown sugar and ginger in a bowl. Add salmon and marinate for ½ hour. Drain salmon. Broil or barbecue fish about 4 inches from heat source. Cook until fish flakes when tested with a fork. Serve with rice and steamed brussel sprouts. Makes 4 servings.

225 calories per serving *7.7 grams fat per serving*
450 mg sodium per serving *75 mg cholesterol per serving*

Substitutions: *sablefish (black cod), mahi mahi, whitefish*

Teriyaki marinade can be reused for up to two weeks if it is refrigerated in airtight containers.

FETTUCINE WITH SALMON

2 tablespoons margarine
1½ cups mushrooms, sliced
2 tablespoons onion, chopped
1 small yellow squash or zucchini, sliced
1 tablespoon flour
⅛ teaspoon dried basil
⅛ teaspoon dried oregano
½ cup skim milk
¾ cup salmon, cooked and flaked, or canned
½ cup frozen peas, thawed
½ cup tomato, diced
1 tablespoon fresh parsley, minced
1 tablespoon white wine
8 oz. fettucine, cooked and drained
pepper to taste
lemon wedges

Melt margarine in skillet. Add mushrooms, onion and squash and saute until tender-crisp. Add flour and herbs; cook and stir 1 minute. Slowly add skim milk, stirring and cooking over medium heat until thickened. Add salmon, peas, tomato, parsley and wine. Heat thoroughly. Toss hot fettucine with vegetable mixture. Season with pepper. Place on warm platter. Garnish with lemon wedges. Makes 6 servings.

270 calories per serving *8 grams fat per serving*
110 mg sodium per serving *40 mg cholesterol per serving*

Substitutions: *canned water-packed tuna, imitation crab, crab meat, cooked shrimp meat*

Excellent use for leftover poached or barbecued salmon.

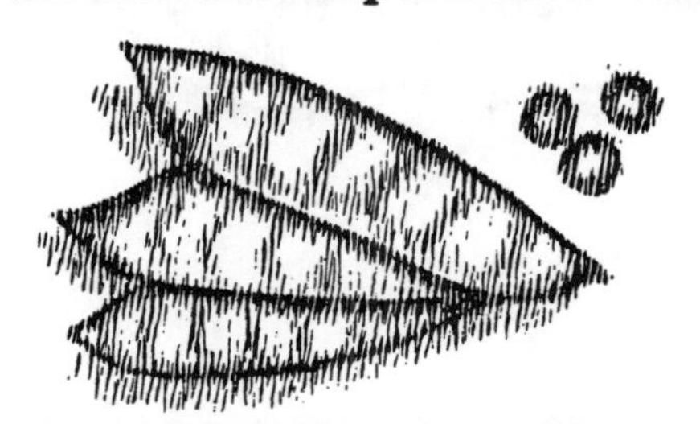

SALMON CURRY PILAF

1 - 15½ oz. can salmon
2 cups cooked rice
1 cup celery, thinly sliced
½ cup parsley, chopped
¼ cup mayonnaise
¼ cup plain low fat yogurt
2 tablespoons lemon juice
1 tablespoon curry powder
paprika

Drain and break salmon into large pieces. Combine rice, celery, parsley and salmon in a medium bowl. Combine mayonnaise, yogurt, lemon juice and curry powder. Add mayonnaise mixture to salmon mixture; toss lightly. Place into 6 lightly-oiled 6 oz. casseroles or custard cups. Sprinkle with paprika. Bake at 400° for 15-20 minutes or until heated. Serve hot with pear salad and whole wheat roll. Makes 8 servings.

190 calories per serving *10 grams fat per serving*
345 mg sodium per serving *30 mg cholesterol per serving*

Substitutions: *bay scallops, cooked shrimp meat, canned water-packed tuna*

A great idea for a potluck dinner.

SALMON IN POTATO SHELLS

3 large baking potatoes
½ cup skim milk
1 - 15½ oz. can salmon
1 teaspoon dried dill weed
1 teaspoon garlic powder
¼ teaspoon pepper
paprika
2 tablespoons part-skim mozzarella cheese, grated

Bake potatoes and cool slightly. Cut in half lengthwise and scoop out cooked potato, leaving shell whole. Beat cooked potato with skim milk until fluffy; add more milk, if necessary. Stir in drained and flaked salmon, dill weed, garlic powder and pepper. Spoon into potato shells and sprinkle with paprika. Return to hot oven and bake until heated through. Top with mozzarella cheese. Makes 6 servings.

185 calories per serving *5.2 grams fat per serving*
325 mg sodium per serving *50 mg cholesterol per serving*

Canned salmon with bones is an excellent source of calcium.

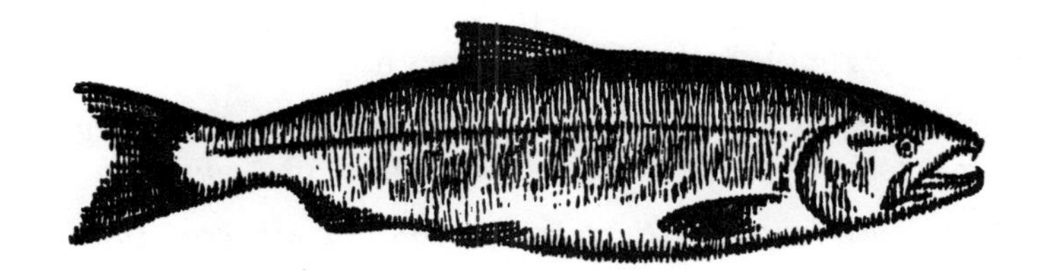

GRILLED SHARK TERIYAKI

1½ lbs. shark steaks
1 - 20 oz. can unsweetened pineapple chunks, drained (reserve juice for marinade)

Marinade:
3 tablespoons pineapple juice
3 tablespoons light soy sauce
2 tablespoons sherry
1 tablespoon fresh ginger, grated
½ teaspoon dry mustard
2 cloves garlic, minced
1 teaspoon brown sugar

1 or 2 large green peppers, cubed

Place shark in a covered 2-quart bowl. Set aside. Drain pineapple, reserving 3 tablespoons of juice; set pineapple chunks aside. To make marinade: in a bowl combine reserved juice, soy sauce, sherry, ginger, mustard, garlic and brown sugar. Stir well. Pour over shark, cover and marinate in refrigerator for 30 minutes, turning once. Using bamboo or metal skewers, make kabobs by alternating pineapple and green pepper. Drain shark, reserving marinade. Place on lightly-oiled grill 4-5 inches from hot charcoals and cook 4-5 minutes (or broil in oven). Baste with marinade and turn. Cook an additional 4-5 minutes or until shark turns opaque. Baste fruit and vegetable kabobs and place on grill. Cook 15-30 seconds on each side or until just browned. Serve with raw carrots and celery and French roll. Makes 4 servings.

250 calories per serving *1.5 grams fat per serving*
625 mg sodium per serving *cholesterol not available*

Substitutions: *swordfish, orange roughy, albacore tuna*

SAN FRANCISCO-STYLE SHARK

2 tablespoons vegetable oil
1 cup mushrooms, sliced
¼ cup onion, chopped
1 clove garlic, minced
1 - 16 oz. can tomatoes, broken up
1 tablespoon parsley, minced
½ teaspoon dried oregano
dash pepper
1 lb. shark fillets

Heat oil in frypan or skillet; add mushrooms, onion and garlic and sauté. Add remaining ingredients, except shark, and bring to a boil. Simmer uncovered, 10 minutes, stirring occasionally. Cut shark into serving-sized pieces and add to tomato mixture. Cover and cook over medium heat 8-10 minutes or until shark turns opaque. Serve with rice. Makes 4 servings.

220 calories per serving *8 grams fat per serving*
670 mg sodium per serving *cholesterol not available*

Substitutions: *swordfish, sea bass, mahi mahi*

PORTUGUESE SKATE WINGS

2 tablespoons margarine, melted
1 cup mushrooms, sliced
1 medium onion, sliced
2 tablespoons flour
½ cup white wine
1 - 20 oz. can tomatoes, undrained
½ teaspoon pepper
¼ teaspoon dried oregano
¼ teaspoon dried thyme
1½ lbs. skate wings

Melt margarine in large skillet. Sauté mushrooms and onion over moderate heat until lightly and evenly browned. Sprinkle flour over mixture in skillet and stir to make smooth paste. Slowly stir in wine. Add tomatoes and seasonings and cook over low heat, stirring constantly, until thickened. Place skate wings in tomato mixture in skillet. Cover and simmer 15 minutes or until fish flakes when tested with a fork. Serve with pasta. Makes 6 servings.

315 calories per serving *7.5 grams fat per serving*
sodium not available *cholesterol not available*

Substitutions: *scallops, rockfish (snapper), flounder*

Skate wings have a delicate and distinctive flavor, much like that of scallops. It is an ideal fish for children and the elderly because it is boneless and easily digested.

SOLE AMANDINE

2 tablespoons margarine, divided
1½ lbs. sole fillets
¼ cup slivered almonds
1 teaspoon lemon peel, grated
2 teaspoons lemon juice
parsley
lemon wedges

In large skillet, over medium heat, melt 1 tablespoon margarine. Sauté the sole fillets for approximately 2 minutes on each side or until fillets just flake when tested with a fork. Transfer to platter and keep warm. In same skillet add remaining 1 tablespoon margarine, almonds, lemon peel and juice. Sauté 1 minute, reducing heat, if necessary, to avoid burning margarine. Pour sauce over fillets. Garnish with parsley and lemon wedges. Serve with boiled new potatoes and Garden Fresh Coleslaw (see page 84). Makes 6 servings.

140 calories per serving *7 grams fat per serving*
95 mg sodium per serving *45 mg cholesterol per serving*

Substitutions: *pollock, cod, orange roughy*

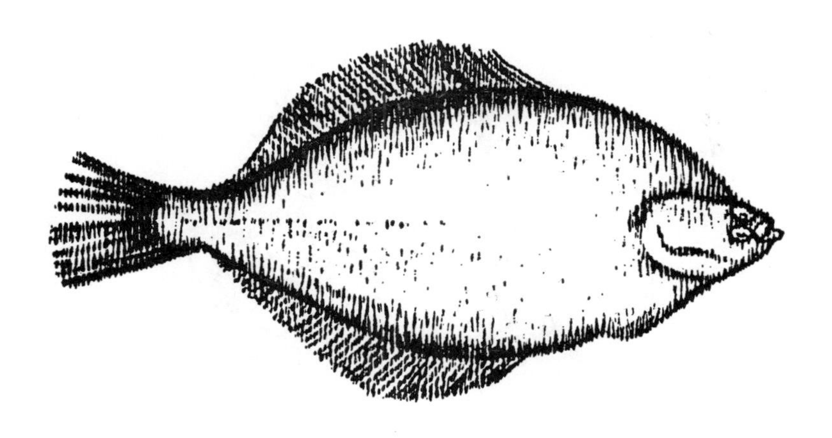

SOLE FILLETS TARRAGON

¼ cup onion, chopped
1 - 10 oz. package frozen vegetable mixture, thawed (broccoli, cauliflower, carrots)
1 lb. sole fillets
pepper to taste
1 teaspoon dried tarragon
1 tablespoon margarine
¼ cup dry white wine
lemon wedges

Combine onion and vegetables and spread over the bottom of an 8x8-inch baking dish. Place fish fillets on top of the vegetables. Sprinkle with pepper and tarragon. Dot with margarine. Pour wine over fish. Bake covered at 400° for 15-20 minutes or until fish flakes when tested with a fork. To serve, lift the fish and vegetables onto a serving platter using a slotted spoon. Garnish with lemon wedges, if desired. Serve with rice and green salad. Makes 4 servings.

180 calories per serving *6 grams fat per serving*
150 mg sodium per serving *50 mg cholesterol per serving*

Substitutions: *hoki, bluefish, rockfish (snapper)*

LEMON-HERBED SOLE

1 lb. sole
pepper to taste
2 tablespoons margarine, melted
1 teaspoon lemon juice
¼ teaspoon lemon peel, grated
⅛ teaspoon dried thyme
¼ cup white wine
1 tablespoon green onion, chopped
2 teaspoons fresh parsley, chopped
3 tablespoons water
1 tablespoon flour
pepper
parsley sprigs
lemon wedges

Sprinkle sole with pepper. In a saucepan combine melted margarine, lemon juice, lemon peel and thyme. Brush over sole placed in lightly-oiled baking dish. Sprinkle with wine, onion and parsley. Bake covered at 400° for 12-15 minutes or until sole flakes when tested with a fork. Transfer to serving platter and keep warm. Combine water, flour and pan drippings in small saucepan. Cook and stir until thickened; pepper to taste. Top each fillet with small amount of sauce; garnish with parsley sprigs and lemon wedges. Pass remaining sauce. Makes 4 servings.

140 calories per serving *6 grams fat per serving*
115 mg sodium per serving *45 mg cholesterol per serving*

***Substitutions:** flounder, orange roughy, cod*

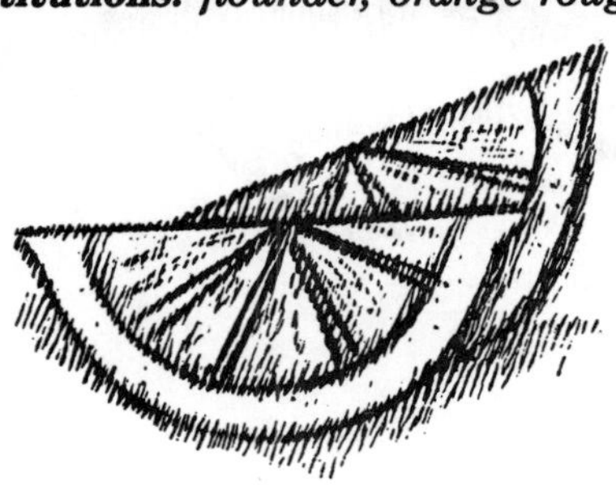

SWORDFISH STEAKS WITH PEPPERCORNS

1 lb. swordfish steaks
1 tablespoon lemon juice
1 garlic clove, minced
1 tablespoon olive oil
1 tablespoon peppercorns, crushed

Place swordfish in pan. Mix lemon juice, garlic and olive oil in small dish and pour over fish. Marinate while crushing peppercorns. Place crushed peppercorns on flat dish. Remove fish from marinade and coat both sides with peppercorns, gently pushing them into flesh of fish. Place fish on broiler pan. Broil 6-10 minutes or until fish turns opaque. Makes 4 servings.

168 calories per serving *8.5 grams fat per serving*
80 mg sodium per serving *57 mg cholesterol per serving*

Substitutions: *ahi (yellowfin tuna), mahi mahi, tilefish*

STIR-FRY SWORDFISH AND VEGETABLES

1 lb. swordfish fillets
pepper to taste
1 tablespoon vegetable oil
2 carrots, diagonally cut in thin slices
1 medium onion, thinly sliced
3 zucchini, cut in ¼-inch slices
¼ teaspoon fresh thyme leaves, crushed

Cut swordfish into 1-inch cubes; sprinkle with pepper and set aside. In hot oil, stir-fry vegetables with thyme until vegetables are tender-crisp. Add fish and stir-fry until fish turns opaque. Serve with brown rice. Makes 4 servings.

200 calories per serving — *10.8 grams fat per serving*
95 mg sodium per serving — *55 mg cholesterol per serving*

Substitutions: *scallops, shark, halibut*

Swordfish, also known as billfish, are found in temperate and tropical seas throughout the world. The average weight is 200-400 pounds but they may reach 1,000 pounds in weight and 15 feet in length. This high-protein fish has a distinctive flavor and firm flesh. Swordfish steaks can be broiled, baked, poached or barbecued. The swordfish catch does not always meet consumer demand, so this fish will remain a high-priced item.

BAKED TILAPIA FILLETS WITH OREGANO

¾ cup fresh bread crumbs
3 tablespoons parsley, minced
1 teaspoon dried oregano
¼ teaspoon garlic powder
¼ teaspoon onion powder
⅛ teaspoon pepper
2 tablespoons vegetable oil
2 lbs. tilapia fillets
1 - 16 oz. can stewed tomatoes

Combine bread crumbs, parsley and seasonings together in a small bowl. Spread 1 tablespoon of oil in the bottom of a baking dish. Place fillets in baking dish. Brush remaining oil on fillets. Sprinkle bread crumb mixture evenly over the fillets. Bake at 500° for 10 minutes. Remove from oven and pour stewed tomatoes over the fillets. Return to oven and bake an additional 10-15 minutes or until fish flakes when tested with a fork. Serve with rice and steamed vegetables. Makes 6 servings.

234 calories per serving *7 grams fat per serving*
142 mg sodium per serving *67 mg cholesterol per serving*

Substitutions: *halibut, orange roughy, cod*

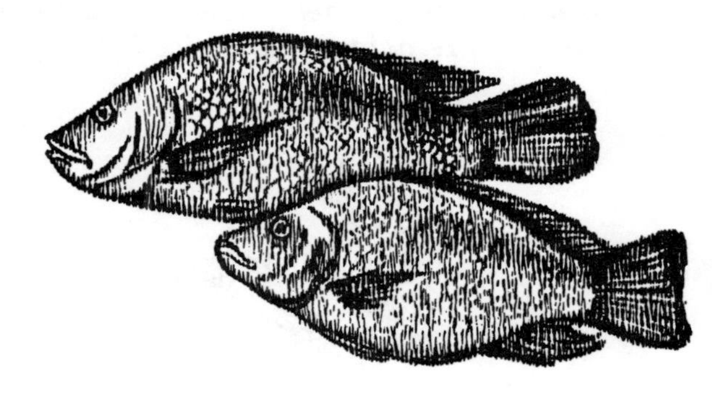

TILEFISH WITH CURRY-YOGURT SAUCE

Curry-Yogurt Sauce:
½ cup orange low fat yogurt or
½ cup plain low fat yogurt with
1 tablespoon orange marmalade
2 teaspoons lime juice
½ teaspoon curry powder

2 tablespoons vegetable oil
2 tablespoons lime juice
1½ lbs. tilefish fillets or steaks

To make Curry-Yogurt Sauce: blend together yogurt, 2 teaspoons lime juice and curry powder. Chill sauce for 15-20 minutes. Combine oil and 2 tablespoons lime juice. Baste fish with oil mixture. Place on lightly-oiled grill 5-6 inches from hot charcoals or broil in oven. Cook 10-15 minutes, turning once and basting frequently until fish flakes when tested with a fork. Serve with Curry-Yogurt Sauce. Garnish with assorted fresh fruit such as strawberries, melon and grapes. Makes 6 servings.

180 calories per serving *4.5 grams fat per serving*
90 mg sodium per serving *80 mg cholesterol per serving*

Substitutions: *lingcod, mahi mahi, shark*

Tilefish is found along the outer edge of the continental shelf from Nova Scotia to Florida and the Gulf of Mexico. Tilefish can grow to over 40 pounds but most weigh from 4-7 pounds. The lean, white flesh is often compared to lobster or scallop meat. The tilefish diet, primarily consisting of red crab and other shellfish, is reflected in its flavor.

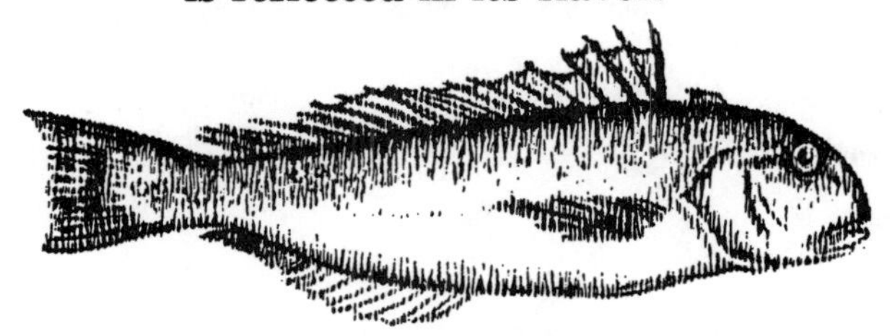

HUKE LODGE BREAKFAST TROUT

2 tablespoons brown sugar
¼ teaspoon salt
2 tablespoons margarine
4 whole dressed trout (approximately 1½ lbs.)

Remove heads of trout if desired. Place sugar and salt in a covered heavy cast-iron pan and slightly burn over heat. Add the margarine and trout; cover and cook over low heat for about 5-10 minutes on each side or until fish flakes when tested with a fork. The trout will have a delicious smokey flavor. Serve with hash browned potatoes and fresh fruit. Makes 4 servings.

270 calories per serving *16.9 grams fat per serving*
255 mg sodium per serving *50 mg cholesterol per serving*

TUNA CHOW MEIN

"Stretch A Can Of Tuna"

1 chicken bouillon cube
1 cup boiling water
1 tablespoon light soy sauce
pepper to taste
1 tablespoon cornstarch
1 tablespoon cold water
2 tablespoons vegetable oil
6 stalks celery, cut diagonally
2 medium onions, chopped
1 - 6 oz. can bamboo shoots, drained
1 green pepper, chopped
⅓ cup mushrooms, sliced
2 cups bean sprouts
1 - 6½ oz. can water-packed tuna, drained and flaked

Dissolve bouillon cube in boiling water; add soy sauce and pepper. Mix cornstarch in cold water until dissolved. Add slowly to bouillon mixture. Set aside. Heat oil in frying pan or wok over high heat. When hot, toss in celery and onion; stir-fry 3 minutes. Add bamboo shoots, green pepper, mushrooms and bean sprouts. Continue to stir-fry 2-3 minutes longer. Stir broth mixture into vegetables. Stir and cook just until sauce is thickened. Add tuna and stir until hot and sauce is clear. Serve immediately over rice. Makes 4 servings.

215 calories per serving *7.5 grams fat per serving*
600 mg sodium per serving *30 mg cholesterol per serving*

Substitution: *canned salmon*

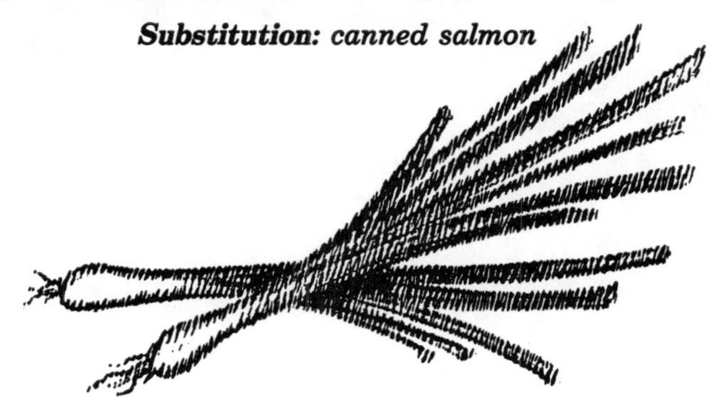

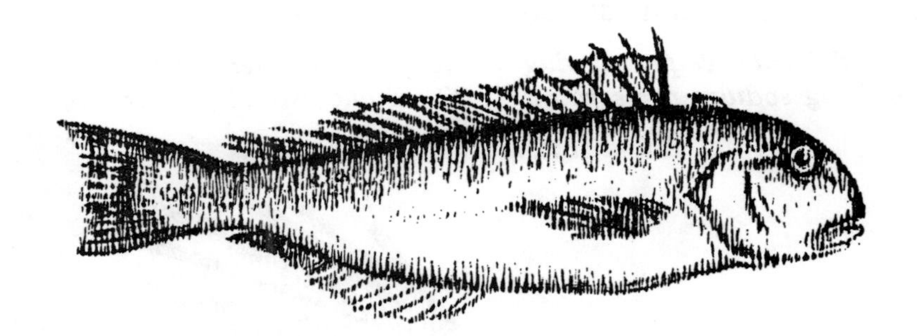

ENTREES:
SHELLFISH

CHAPTER 6

ENTREES: SHELLFISH

LINGUINI WITH CLAM SAUCE

6 ripe tomatoes, medium size
2 tablespoons fresh parsley, chopped
1 teaspoon dried basil
2 tablespoons lemon juice
1 clove garlic, minced
¼ teaspoon pepper
1 lb. clams, minced
1 lb. linguini or other pasta
Parmesan cheese, grated

Dip tomatoes in boiling water until skin comes off easily, about 30 seconds. Peel and chop. Combine tomatoes with parsley, basil, lemon juice, garlic, pepper and clams in a saucepan. Bring to boil. Reduce heat and simmer uncovered 15-20 minutes. Stir occasionally. Cook pasta in boiling water following package directions and drain. Return to kettle and toss with about ⅓ of the sauce. Divide among 6 deep plates. Top with remaining sauce and serve at once. Sprinkle with Parmesan cheese if desired. Serve with green salad and French bread. Makes 6 servings.

Sauce:

90 calories per serving *2.9 grams fat per serving*
65 mg sodium per serving *30 mg cholesterol per serving*

Substitutions: *chopped squid, cooked shrimp meat*

CLAMS MOZZARELLA

1½ lbs. clams, chopped
2 tablespoons parsley, finely chopped
2 tablespoons chives, chopped
2 cloves garlic, finely minced
dash cayenne pepper
dash pepper
12 oz. part-skim mozzarella cheese, shredded
6 slices pumpernickel bread

Sauté clams with parsley, chives, garlic and peppers in pan for 2-3 minutes. Spoon clam mixture into a bowl and toss with mozzarella cheese. Line bottom of 9x13-inch pan with bread, and spoon clam and cheese mixture evenly over bread. Broil until golden brown and bubbly. Cut into serving-sized pieces. Serve immediately. This makes a wonderful lunch entrée or can be served at buffets or potluck dinners. It also makes a wonderful appetizer. For individual appetizers, spread clam and cheese mixture over snack-sized bread slices and heat under broiler. Makes 6 servings.

290 calories per serving *2.3 grams fat per serving*
530 mg sodium per serving *360 mg cholesterol per serving*

Substitution: *chopped squid*

MARYLAND CRAB CAKES

¼ cup non-fat quark
or processed low fat cottage cheese
1 teaspoon lemon juice
2 teaspoons Worcestershire sauce
dash celery salt
dash pepper
dash ginger
dash paprika
dash dry mustard
4 - 6 dashes hot pepper sauce (Tabasco)
1 egg, lightly beaten
½ cup soft bread crumbs
8 oz. crab meat, flaked
¼ cup onion, finely chopped
¼ cup celery, finely chopped
¼ cup dry bread crumbs
2 teaspoons vegetable oil

Blend quark, lemon juice, Worcestershire sauce, seasonings and Tabasco in a bowl until smooth. Add remaining ingredients except bread crumbs and oil. Mix well. Cover tightly and refrigerate until well-chilled. Divide chilled mixture into 4 patties. Put bread crumbs in a bowl. Coat patties with crumbs. Heat oil in non-stick skillet over medium heat. Add crab cakes and cook until brown on both sides. Makes 4 servings.

166 calories per serving *4 grams fat per serving*
343 mg sodium per serving *142 mg cholesterol per serving*

Substitutions: *cooked, flaked lingcod, pollock or walleye pike*

SWEET POTATO CRAB CAKES

½ cup cooked sweet potatoes, whipped
2 teaspoons lemon juice
2 tablespoons lite mayonnaise
1 tablespoon onion, finely chopped
3 tablespoons celery, finely chopped
¼ teaspoon garlic powder
1 lb. crab meat
pepper to taste
1 tablespoon olive oil
½ cup Panko breading or seasoned bread crumbs

Whip sweet potatoes in large bowl. Add lemon juice, mayonnaise, onion, celery, garlic powder and pepper and blend. Add crab and mix all ingredients together. Form crab cake mixture into 8 patties. Place breading in bowl and coat crab cakes. Heat olive oil in non-stick skillet over medium heat. Sauté crab cakes until golden brown. Makes 4 servings or 8 crab cakes.

216 calories per serving *8 grams fat per serving*
444 mg sodium per serving *90 mg cholesterol per serving*

Substitutions: *cooked, flaked walleye pike or lingcod*

CRAB BROCCOLI CASSEROLE

1 - 10 oz. package frozen broccoli spears
2 tablespoons margarine
2 tablespoons flour
1 cup skim milk
dash pepper
dash paprika
6 oz. crab meat
¼ cup green onion, thinly sliced
1 tablespoon pimiento, coarsely chopped
2 tablespoons slivered almonds

Thaw broccoli and cut stems in bite-sized pieces, keeping flowerets separate. Make white sauce by melting margarine in small saucepan; slowly stir in flour, then skim milk. Cook over moderate heat until thickened, stirring constantly. Fold in crab meat, onion and pimiento. Arrange broccoli flowerets around edge of an 8x8-inch baking dish. Fill center with remaining broccoli pieces and spoon sauce over broccoli in center of casserole. Sprinkle nuts over top. Bake at 375° for 20 minutes or until hot and bubbly. Serve with fruit salad and whole wheat bread. Makes 4 servings.

160 calories per serving *6.7 grams fat per serving*
240 mg sodium per serving *45 mg cholesterol per serving*

Substitutions: *imitation crab, cooked shrimp meat*

Make this entrée ahead of time and refrigerate.
Add 5 - 10 minutes to cooking time.

CRAB WITH RED SAUCE

1 tablespoon margarine
2 tablespoons onion, minced
1 clove garlic, minced
1 - 8 oz. can tomato sauce
¼ cup catsup
¼ teaspoon dried oregano
1½ lbs. crab meat

Melt margarine in skillet. Add onion and garlic and sauté until tender; stir in remaining ingredients. Simmer 5 minutes. Serve over fettucine noodles. Makes 6 servings.

130 calories per serving — *3.2 grams fat per serving*
620 mg sodium per serving — *90 mg cholesterol per serving*

Substitutions: *imitation crab, cooked shrimp meat or lobster meat*

MUSSELS IN TOMATO SAUCE

36 mussels in shells
2 teaspoons vegetable oil
⅓ cup green onion, sliced
¼ cup green pepper, diced
¼ cup red bell pepper, diced
1 - 14½ oz. can whole tomatoes, undrained
½ cup tomato sauce
½ teaspoon dried thyme
½ teaspoon dried basil
¼ teaspoon garlic powder
¼ teaspoon paprika
½ cup white wine
1 bay leaf

Debeard mussels and scrub under cold running water. Heat oil in a large skillet over medium heat. Add onion, green and red peppers and sauté until vegetables are tender-crisp. Add tomatoes, tomato sauce, thyme, basil, garlic powder and paprika and stir well. Reduce heat and simmer uncovered 25 minutes or until thickened, stirring frequently. Add wine and bay leaf and bring to a boil. Add mussels and cook 2 minutes or until shells open. Discard bay leaf. Spoon sauce onto serving platter. Arrange mussels over sauce. Serve with vegetable salad and French bread. Makes 4 servings.

139 calories per serving *2 grams fat per serving*
388 mg sodium per serving *29 mg cholesterol per serving*

Substitution: *clams in shell*

STEAMED MUSSELS OR CLAMS

36 mussels or steamer clams in shells
2 tablespoons margarine
1 cup white wine
½ cup green onion, chopped
¼ cup parsley, chopped
2 cloves garlic, minced

Scrub clams or debeard mussels. (To debeard mussels, clip beard off with scissors just before cooking.) Melt margarine with wine in 8-quart saucepan. Add green onion, parsley and garlic to wine sauce. Place clams or mussels in saucepan. Cover with tight lid. Steam on medium heat for approximately 10 minutes or until shells open. Shake the pan during this time to cook the clams or mussels evenly. The broth is delicious to drink. Makes 2 servings.

360 calories per serving *15 grams fat per serving*
495 mg sodium per serving *60 mg cholesterol per serving*

Substitutions: *crawfish, scallops in shell*

A delicious appetizer for 6.

BARBECUED OYSTERS IN THE SHELL

Oysters in shell
12 large, 20 medium, or 32 small

Snappy Barbecue Sauce (see page 238)
or
Barbecue Basting Sauce (see page 239)

Scrub oyster shells thoroughly. Place oysters on a barbecue grill, lid side up*, about 4 inches from hot charcoals. Barbecue 5-10 minutes or until shells begin to open. (The larger the oyster, the longer the cooking time.) Some oysters may need a gentle nudge to open. Place a knife under the lid of the oyster and pry the shells apart. Snappy Barbecue Sauce (see page 238) or Barbecue Basting Sauce (see page 239) may be served with the oysters. Makes 4 servings.

90 calories per serving | *2.5 grams fat per serving*
90 mg sodium per serving | *45 mg cholesterol per serving*

****Oysters in the shell have two sides. The lid of the oyster is flat. The cup of the oyster is bowl shaped. In order to retain the juice in the oyster be sure to place oysters on the grill with the lid side up.***

FISHERMAN'S CHOICE OYSTERS

1 lb. oysters, shucked or 2 - 8 oz. jars small oysters
2 tablespoons margarine
1 teaspoon dried dill weed
lemon wedges

Shuck, drain and dry oysters on a paper towel. Place them on a cooking sheet. Melt margarine; add dill weed and brush over oysters. Broil about 3 minutes, until lightly browned, turning once. Serve with Zesty Cocktail Sauce (see page 235) and lemon wedges. Makes 4 servings.

130 calories per serving | *6.8 grams fat per serving*
155 mg sodium per serving | *60 mg cholesterol per serving*

Oysters are an excellent source of iron and zinc.

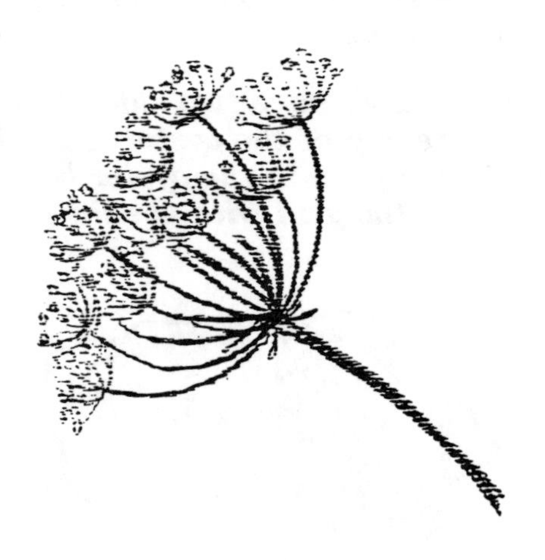

BROILED SCALLOP SAUTERNE

1 lb. scallops
1 tablespoon lemon juice
1 teaspoon dried thyme
½ teaspoon dried dill weed
2 tablespoons sauterne
2 teaspoons fresh parsley, chopped
lemon wedges

Sprinkle scallops with lemon juice, thyme, dill weed and sauterne in a bowl. Toss lightly. Place on broiler pan. Broil 3-4 minutes. Sprinkle with parsley and serve with lemon wedges. Makes 4 servings.

97 calories per serving — *2.5 grams fat per serving*
290 mg sodium per serving — *55 mg cholesterol per serving*

Substitutions: *oysters, monkfish medallions, halibut cubes*

All scallops are the same biologically but vary in size. They are grouped into three categories based on size:
Sea scallops — 10-40 scallops per pound
Bay scallops — 40-100 scallops per pound
Calico scallops — over 100 scallops per pound

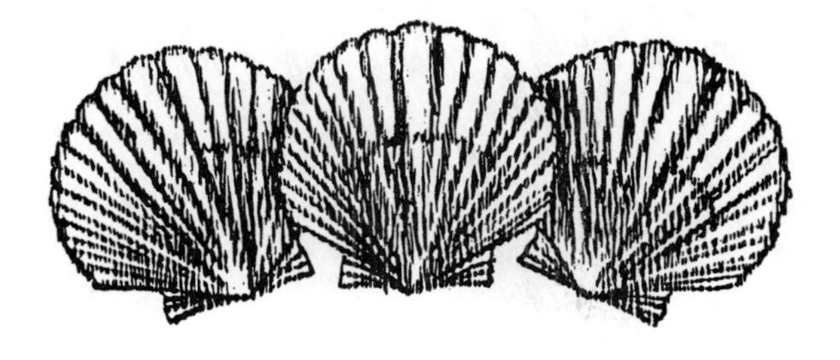

SCALLOP SAUTÉ

1 lb. scallops
2 tablespoons flour
2 tablespoons margarine
¼ cup green onion, minced
1 clove garlic, minced
½ cup mushrooms, thinly sliced
¼ cup sherry
pepper to taste
parsley

Dust scallops very lightly with flour. In a large frying pan heat margarine. Add onion, garlic and mushrooms. Sauté until the mushrooms are tender. Add scallops and sherry; cook at a very high heat until sherry is reduced by half. When finished, there should be only a very light brown sauce glazing the scallops. Pepper to taste. Serve with rice sprinkled with parsley and a green salad. Makes 4 servings.

150 calories per serving *6.5 grams fat per serving*
660 mg sodium per serving *90 mg cholesterol per serving*

Substitutions: *monkfish medallions, halibut cubes, peeled and deveined shrimp (prawns)*

NORTHWEST BROILED SHRIMP (PRAWNS)

1 lb. shrimp (prawns), peeled and deveined
2 tablespoons margarine, melted
1 tablespoon lemon juice
¼ teaspoon paprika
¼ teaspoon garlic powder
fresh parsley, chopped

Arrange shrimp over bottom of a heat-proof dish. Combine remaining ingredients except parsley. Spoon half of mixture over shrimp. Broil 3-6 minutes or until shrimp turn pink. Baste occasionally with remaining mixture. Sprinkle with parsley before serving. Makes 4 servings.

160 calories per serving *6.4 grams fat per serving*
225 mg sodium per serving *180 mg cholesterol per serving*

Substitutions: *oysters, scallops, swordfish*

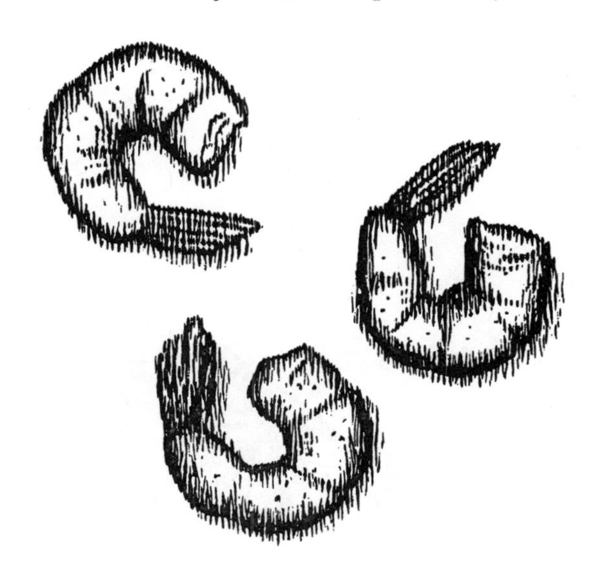

POACHED SHRIMP (PRAWNS)

1 quart water
1 small lemon, sliced or 2 tablespoons lemon juice
1 small onion, sliced
2 teaspoons pickling spices
¼ teaspoon salt (optional)
1½ lbs. shrimp (prawns)

Combine water with lemon, onion and spices. Bring to a boil and add shrimp (prawns). Cover and simmer 3 minutes. Drain and cool. Remove shells. Use in recipe calling for cooked prawns or shrimp. Makes 4 servings.

165 calories per serving 1.4 grams fat per serving
235 mg sodium per serving (calculated without salt)
265 mg cholesterol per serving

Substitutions: *cod, halibut, haddock*

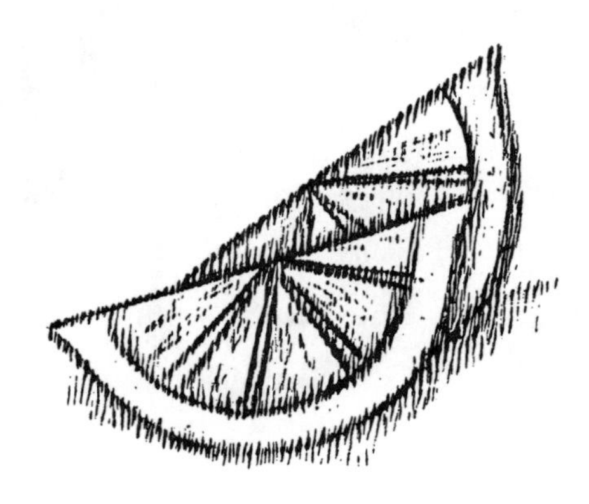

SHRIMP (PRAWNS) IN BEER

3 cups beer
1 cup water
1 bay leaf
1½ lbs. shrimp (prawns)

Bring beer, water and bay leaf to a boil. Add shrimp (prawns). Cover and simmer 5 minutes. Drain. Remove shells. Serve warm or chilled. Makes 4 servings.

180 calories per serving *1.4 grams fat per serving*
240 mg sodium per serving *265 mg cholesterol per serving*

Substitutions: *salmon, albacore tuna, sablefish (black cod)*

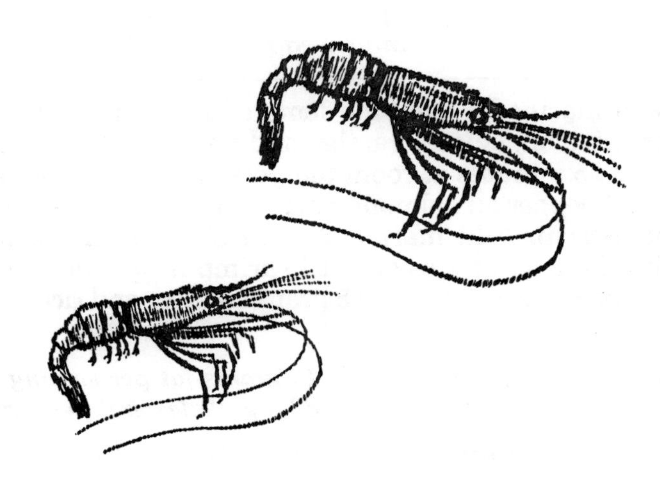

ALMOND SHRIMP (PRAWNS) AND PEPPERS

Marinade:
2 tablespoons lemon juice
3 cloves garlic, finely minced
⅛ teaspoon cayenne pepper
½ teaspoon pepper
1 tablespoon olive oil
2 tablespoons chives, thinly sliced, or
2 teaspoons dried chives
2 tablespoons fresh parsley, chopped
2 teaspoons dried basil

1½ lbs. medium, raw shrimp (prawns), peeled and deveined
1 red bell pepper, julienne cut
½ cup slivered almonds
1 tablespoon margarine
lemon wedges

To make marinade: combine lemon juice, garlic, cayenne, pepper, olive oil, chives, parsley and basil. Add shrimp and marinate 15 minutes at room temperature. In wok or skillet sauté bell pepper and almonds in margarine until bell pepper is tender-crisp. Add marinade with shrimp and continue sautéing for 2-3 minutes or until shrimp is opaque. Garnish with lemon wedges. Serve with grape clusters and rice. Makes 6 servings.

160 calories per serving *10 grams fat per serving*
180 mg sodium per serving *180 mg cholesterol per serving*

Substitutions: *scallops, halibut cheeks*

GINGERED SHRIMP (PRAWNS) ON SKEWERS

Marinade:
2 tablespoons lemon juice
2 tablespoons sesame oil
2 tablespoons green onion, minced
1 teaspoon fresh ginger, grated or
¼ teaspoon ground ginger

1 lb. (about 40) medium-sized shrimp (prawns), peeled and deveined
8 crisp romaine lettuce leaves
lemon wedges
1 large cucumber, cut into ¼-inch thick slices

To make marinade: in a bowl combine lemon juice, sesame oil, green onion and ginger. Place shrimp in bowl and marinate for 30 minutes at room temperature. Remove shrimp from marinade and place on skewers. Broil 2-3 minutes. Garnish plate with lettuce leaves and lemon wedges. Arrange cucumber slices on lettuce leaves and place skewered shrimp on plate. Serve with rice. Makes 4 servings.

170 calories per serving *7.9 grams fat per serving*
160 mg sodium per serving *180 mg cholesterol per serving*

Substitutions: *scallops, monkfish medallions*

STIR-FRIED SQUID (CALAMARI)

1¼ lbs. whole squid

Marinade:
2 tablespoons light soy sauce
⅛ teaspoon pepper
2 tablespoons white wine
2 teaspoons cornstarch
1 tablespoon sesame oil

1 tablespoon vegetable oil
1 teaspoon fresh ginger, grated
2 cloves garlic, minced
½ cup mushrooms, sliced
½ medium red or green pepper, cut into thin strips
¼ cup green onion, sliced
½ cup peas, frozen

Clean squid. Cut mantles (bodies) widthwise into ¼-inch strips; chop tentacles. To make marinade: combine soy sauce, pepper, wine, cornstarch and sesame oil; mix well. Add squid. Marinate at room temperature while preparing remaining ingredients. In large skillet or wok, heat oil. Add ginger and garlic; stir-fry for 30 seconds. Add squid and vegetables with marinade; stir-fry briefly until squid is just cooked through, approximately 45 seconds. Serve immediately over hot rice. Makes 4 servings.

200 calories per serving *8 grams fat per serving*
550 mg sodium per serving *265 mg cholesterol per serving*

CHAPTER SEVEN

MICROWAVE

CHAPTER 7

MICROWAVE

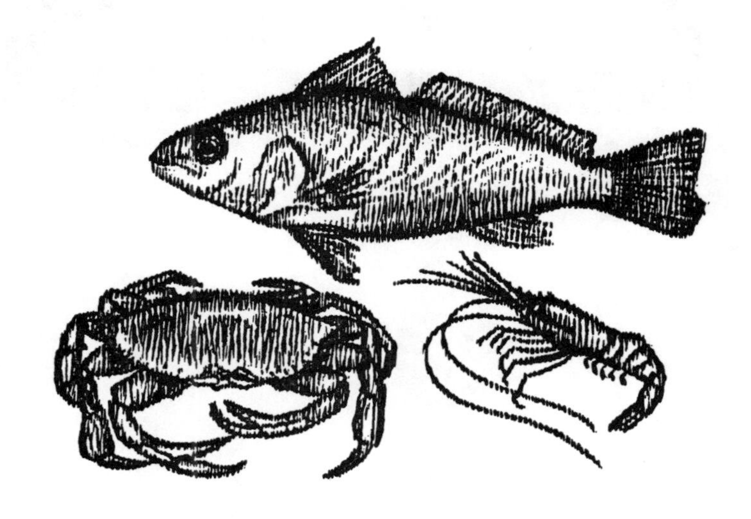

STEAMED BLUEFISH WITH ORANGE SAUCE

1 lb. bluefish fillets
1 tablespoon margarine, melted
2 tablespoons orange juice
2 teaspoons orange rind, grated
⅛ teaspoon nutmeg
⅛ teaspoon pepper

MICROWAVE METHOD:
Place fillets in microwave-proof baking dish. Set aside. In bowl combine remaining ingredients; pour over bluefish. Cover with plastic wrap and microwave on HIGH for 3 minutes. Rotate dish ¼-turn and microwave on HIGH for 2 minutes until fish just flakes when tested with a fork. Remove from oven and let stand to complete cooking. Makes 4 servings.

170 calories per serving — *7.5 grams fat per serving*
104 mg sodium per serving — *67 mg cholesterol per serving*

Substitutions: *sturgeon, salmon, sablefish (black cod)*

SPANISH-STYLE COD

½ lb. cod fillets
pepper
⅓ cup onion, chopped
3 tablespoons green chiles, diced
1 tablespoon vegetable oil
1 tomato, chopped
¼ cup fresh parsley, chopped
1 tablespoon lime juice
¼ teaspoon dried oregano
dash sugar
4 green pepper rings
lime wedges

MICROWAVE METHOD:
Sprinkle cod with pepper. Place in microwave-proof baking dish. Set aside. Combine onion, chiles, oil, tomato, parsley, lime juice, oregano and sugar in a microwave-proof bowl. Microwave on HIGH for two minutes. Arrange green pepper rings over cod and pour tomato mixture over all; cover with plastic wrap. Microwave at HIGH 3 minutes. Rotate dish ¼ turn; microwave at HIGH 3-4 minutes longer or until cod just flakes when tested with a fork. Remove from oven and let stand to complete cooking.

CONVENTIONAL METHOD:
Sprinkle cod with pepper. Sauté onion and chiles in oil. Add tomato, parsley, lime juice, oregano and sugar. Arrange green pepper rings on fillets in baking dish. Pour tomato mixture over fish. Bake at 400° for 10 minutes or until fish flakes when tested with a fork. Serve with rice; garnish with lime wedges. Makes 2 servings.

200 calories per serving *8 grams fat per serving*
100 mg sodium per serving *50 mg cholesterol per serving*

Substitutions: *orange roughy, pollock, halibut*

SPEEDY POACHED FLOUNDER

1 lb. flounder fillets
½ cup white wine
¼ teaspoon pepper
¼ teaspoon dried dill weed

MICROWAVE METHOD:
Place fish fillets in microwave-proof dish. Pour wine over fish fillets. Sprinkle with pepper and dill weed. Cover with plastic wrap. Microwave on HIGH for 3-6 minutes or until fish just flakes when tested with a fork. Remove from oven and let stand to complete cooking. Serve with microwaved potatoes and vegetables. Makes 4 servings.

115 calories per serving *1 gram fat per serving*
80 mg sodium per serving *55 mg cholesterol per serving*

Substitutions: *hoki, pollock, sole*

The myth that seafood from salt water is high in salt (sodium) is not true. Fresh or frozen seafood without breading or sauce is low in sodium.

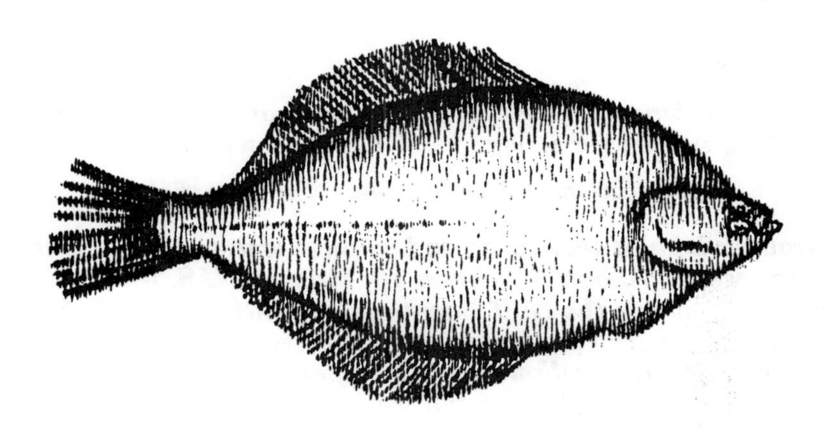

AFTER WORK GROUPER (CHILEAN SEA BASS)

1 lb. grouper
1½ tablespoons margarine, melted
¼ cup dry bread crumbs
1 tablespoon fresh parsley, chopped
⅛ teaspoon pepper
⅛ teaspoon paprika
lemon wedges

MICROWAVE METHOD:
Cut grouper into serving-sized pieces. Coat on all sides with margarine. Place in microwave-proof dish. Combine bread crumbs, parsley and seasonings. Sprinkle crumb mixture over grouper. Cover with paper towel; microwave on HIGH for 2 minutes. Rotate dish ¼ turn; microwave on HIGH 1-2 minutes longer or until grouper just flakes when tested with a fork. Remove from oven and let stand to complete cooking. Serve with lemon wedges. Makes 4 servings.

CONVENTIONAL METHOD:
Cut grouper into serving-sized pieces. Coat on all sides with melted margarine. Place on broiling pan. Combine bread crumbs, parsley and seasonings. Sprinkle crumb mixture over grouper. Broil for 10 minutes or until grouper flakes when tested with a fork. Serve with lemon wedges. Makes 4 servings.

160 calories per serving *5.4 grams fat per serving*
145 mg sodium per serving *57 mg cholesterol per serving*

Substitutions: *Northern pike, catfish, bluefish*

Grouper inhabit temperate and tropical waters throughout the world. About 70 species are found in U.S. waters, primarily along the Gulf Coast and Atlantic states. Other names for grouper include Chilean sea bass, jewfish, black grouper, yellowmouth grouper and red grouper. The largest grouper can weigh in excess of 600 pounds. The white flesh is ideal for poaching, steaming, broiling and barbecuing.

CITRUS-BAKED HADDOCK

½ lb. haddock fillets
pepper
1 tablespoon lemon juice
1 teaspoon vegetable oil
½ medium onion, sliced in thin rings
1 small orange, peeled and sliced
2 teaspoons fresh parsley, minced

MICROWAVE METHOD:
Sprinkle haddock with pepper. Combine lemon juice and oil in microwave-proof baking dish; turn fish to coat all sides with lemon-oil mixture. Arrange onion slices over fish. Cover with plastic wrap; microwave on HIGH 2 minutes. Remove cover and arrange orange slices over onion; sprinkle with parsley and cover. Rotate dish ¼ turn; microwave on HIGH 2-3 minutes longer or until fish just flakes when tested with a fork. Let stand to complete cooking. Makes 2 servings.

CONVENTIONAL METHOD:
Sprinkle haddock with pepper. Combine lemon juice and oil; brush on all sides of fish. Place fish in baking dish and arrange onion rings over fish; brush with remaining lemon-oil mixture. Bake at 400° for 5 minutes. Arrange orange slices over onion; sprinkle with parsley. Bake 5-8 minutes longer or until fish flakes when tested with a fork. Makes 2 servings.

130 calories per serving — *4.5 grams fat per serving*
60 mg sodium per serving — *60 mg cholesterol per serving*

Substitutions: *cod, orange roughy, halibut*

HALIBUT ON A BED OF VEGETABLES

¼ cup lemon juice
1 tablespoon olive oil
1 small zucchini, cut into rounds
½ red bell pepper, cut into strips
1 plum tomato, diced
¼ cup parsley or cilantro, chopped
pepper to taste
½ lb. halibut

MICROWAVE METHOD:
Place lemon juice and oil in a microwave-proof baking dish. Add zucchini and red pepper, stir well and cook, covered, 2½ minutes. Stir in tomato, parsley and pepper. Add halibut. Spoon half of liquid and vegetable mixture over fish and cook, covered, 4-5 minutes or until fish just flakes when tested with a fork. Let stand to complete cooking. Makes 2 servings.

266 calories per serving *8.7 grams fat per serving*
80 mg sodium per serving *92 mg cholesterol per serving*

Substitutions: *sole, scallops, trout fillets*

CANTONESE-STYLE LINGCOD

1 lb. lingcod fillets
1 tablespoon margarine
2 teaspoons lemon juice
pepper

Sauce:
1 tablespoon packed brown sugar
2 teaspoons cornstarch
2 tablespoons each water and cider vinegar
1 tablespoon light soy sauce
1 cup celery, diagonally sliced
½ cup canned unsweetened pineapple chunks, drained

MICROWAVE METHOD:
Cut cod into serving-sized pieces; place in microwave-proof dish. Dot with margarine; sprinkle with lemon juice. Season with pepper. Cover with plastic wrap; microwave on HIGH 2 minutes. Rotate dish ¼ turn; microwave on HIGH 1-2 minutes longer or until cod just flakes when tested with a fork. Remove from microwave oven and keep cod covered while preparing sauce. To make sauce: combine brown sugar and cornstarch in microwave-proof bowl; add cold water, vinegar and soy sauce. Microwave on HIGH 1 minute or until thickened. Stir once during cooking. Stir in celery and pineapple. Microwave on HIGH 2 minutes. Serve over cod with rice. Makes 4 servings.

135 calories per serving *3.6 grams fat per serving*
325 mg sodium per serving *45 mg cholesterol per serving*

Substitutions: *rockfish (snapper), cod, halibut*

The lingcod is neither a ling nor a cod, but a member of the greenling family. Lingcod vary in weight from 5-20 pounds. They range from the Baja Peninsula of Mexico to Northwest Alaska but are most abundant in the colder waters of the north. The fillets are white, medium firm in texture, and have a delicious flavor.

SALMON WITH CUCUMBER SAUCE

1 medium onion, thinly sliced
1 lemon, thinly sliced
1 clove garlic, minced
¼ teaspoon dried dill weed
¼ teaspoon salt
1½ lbs. salmon fillets, boneless
¼ cup mayonnaise
¼ cup plain low fat yogurt
¼ cucumber, peeled and finely chopped

MICROWAVE METHOD:
Spread onion, lemon, garlic and spices in bottom of baking dish. Arrange salmon on top, thickest portions toward outside of dish. Cover tightly with plastic wrap. Microwave 5 minutes on HIGH. Mix mayonnaise, plain low fat yogurt and cucumber and spread over salmon. Microwave on HIGH until fish just flakes when tested with a fork. Let stand to complete cooking. Garnish with lemon twists and parsley sprigs. Makes 6 servings.

240 calories per serving — *15 grams fat per serving*
200 mg sodium per serving — *70 mg cholesterol per serving*

Substitutions: *trout fillets, catfish, rockfish (snapper)*

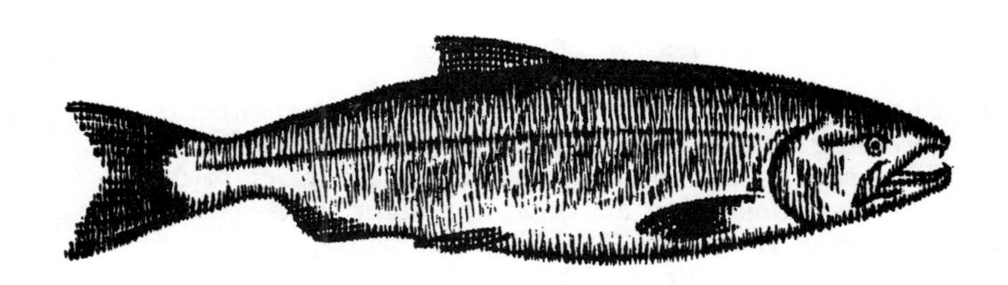

SWORDFISH WITH BASIL

1 lb. swordfish steaks
¼ cup white wine
1 tablespoon fresh basil, chopped
or 1 teaspoon dried basil
1 teaspoon olive oil
¼ teaspoon pepper
2 cloves garlic, minced
4 thin slices of red onion
½ lemon, thinly sliced

MICROWAVE METHOD:
Place fish in a microwave-proof baking dish. Combine wine, basil, olive oil, pepper and garlic in a small bowl and stir together; pour over fish. Cover and marinate in refrigerator 15 minutes, turning fish once. Drain, reserving marinade. Place fish in microwave-proof baking dish. Spoon marinade over fish. Top with onion slices, separated into rings, and lemon slices. Cover with plastic wrap. Microwave on HIGH for 3-5 minutes or until fish just turns opaque. Let stand to complete cooking. Makes 4 servings.

160 calories per serving *6 grams fat per serving*
80 mg sodium per serving *57 mg cholesterol per serving*

Substitutions: *salmon, walleye pike, albacore tuna*

OPENING-DAY TROUT

1 whole trout, about 6 oz.
½ tablespoon margarine
1 slice onion
1 slice lemon
pepper to taste

MICROWAVE METHOD:
Dress trout; remove head and tail, and fillet if desired. Place margarine, onion, lemon and pepper in inner cavity and secure with a toothpick. Place trout in baking dish with backbone facing outward and cover with plastic wrap. Microwave on HIGH for 2½-3½ minutes or until trout just flakes when tested with a fork. Let stand to complete cooking. Makes 1 serving.

For: 2 trout microwave 5-7 minutes;
3 trout microwave 7½-10 minutes;
4 trout microwave 10-14 minutes.

245 calories per serving — *16.9 grams fat per serving*
122 mg sodium per serving — *50 mg cholesterol per serving*

Substitutions: *whiting, pollock, bluefish*

If there is a lingering odor in your microwave after cooking seafood, boil half of a fresh lemon for 5 minutes in water in the microwave. The fresh lemon aroma will freshen up the microwave.

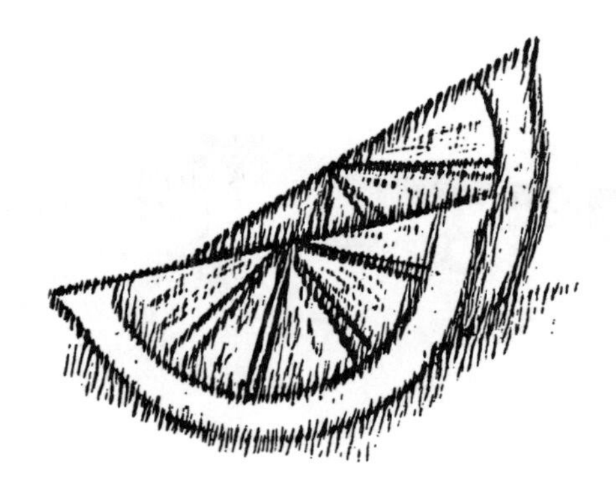

THREE-MINUTE STEAMED CLAMS

"A Meal In A Hurry"

24 large or 45 small clams in shells
½ cup water

MICROWAVE METHOD:
Wash shellfish thoroughly, discarding any broken or open shells. Set aside. Pour water into a 2-quart casserole; cover. Microwave on HIGH until water boils. Add shellfish and cover. Microwave on HIGH until shellfish open, 3-4 minutes, stirring about halfway through the cooking time. Serve with Barbecue Basting Sauce (see page 239), hot French bread, cucumber slices and pineapple chunks. Makes 4 servings.

90 calories per serving *2 grams fat per serving*
90 mg sodium per serving *40 mg cholesterol per serving*

Substitutions: *oysters or mussels in shell*

MICKEY'S FAVORITE OYSTERS

1 - 8 oz. jar medium-size oysters
½ tablespoon margarine, melted
2 tablespoons dry seasoned bread crumbs
¼ teaspoon garlic powder
2 tablespoons dry sherry
1 tablespoon lemon juice
1 tablespoon Parmesan cheese

MICROWAVE METHOD:
Wash oysters under cold running water. Place on paper towels and pat dry. Combine melted margarine, bread crumbs, garlic powder, sherry and lemon juice in small bowl. Place oysters on microwave-proof platter. Spread margarine mixture over oysters. Cover with plastic wrap and microwave on HIGH for 3 minutes. Remove plastic wrap. Sprinkle Parmesan cheese over oysters. Return, uncovered, to microwave and cook on HIGH for 30 seconds or until done. Makes 2 servings.

CONVENTIONAL METHOD:
Prepare margarine mixture and oysters as instructed above. Place oysters in baking dish and spread margarine mixture over oysters. Bake uncovered at 400° for 4-5 minutes. Sprinkle Parmesan cheese over oysters. Bake 1 minute or until done. Makes 2 servings.

159 calories per serving *5 grams fat per serving*
243 mg sodium per serving *59 mg cholesterol per serving*

Substitutions: *mussels or clams on the half shell, scallops*

MICROWAVE SHRIMP (PRAWNS)

2 tablespoons margarine
2 tablespoons dried parsley
2 tablespoons lemon juice
1 clove garlic, minced
¼ cup white wine
1 lb. raw jumbo shrimp (prawns), peeled and deveined
paprika

MICROWAVE METHOD:
Place margarine in 2-quart casserole. Microwave on HIGH until melted, about 30 seconds. Stir in parsley, lemon juice, garlic and wine. Add seafood; toss to coat. Cover dish. Microwave on HIGH until seafood turns pink, about 1-2 minutes. Sprinkle with paprika. Serve with fruit compote and rice. Makes 4 servings.

165 calories per serving *6.5 grams fat per serving*
230 mg sodium per serving *180 mg cholesterol per serving*

Substitutions: *scallops, halibut, salmon*

STUFFED JUMBO SHRIMP (SCAMPI)

2 lbs. large shrimp or scampi, in the shell
1 tablespoon margarine
¼ cup celery, finely chopped
1 small onion, finely chopped
1 tablespoon margarine, melted
½ cup dry bread crumbs
¼ teaspoon dried basil
½ teaspoon fresh parsley, chopped
¼ teaspoon garlic salt

MICROWAVE METHOD:
Peel shrimp, leaving shell on tail section. Lay on back. With a sharp knife, split almost through (butterfly cut). Devein. Set aside. Combine celery, onion and margarine in a 1-quart casserole. Microwave 3 minutes on HIGH or until onion is transparent. Stir in remaining ingredients. Brush shrimp with melted margarine. Spoon 1 tablespoon of mixture into butterflied area of shrimp. Place in baking dish with tail in center of dish. Microwave 3 minutes on HIGH or until shrimp are pink. Do not overcook. Time varies slightly with size of shrimp. Makes 4 servings.

200 calories per serving — *8 grams fat per serving*
425 mg sodium per serving — *160 mg cholesterol per serving*

***Substitution:** lobster tails*

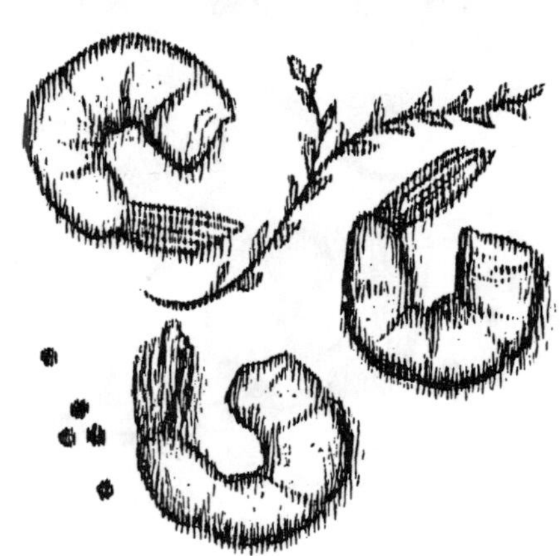

CHAPTER EIGHT

COMPANY'S

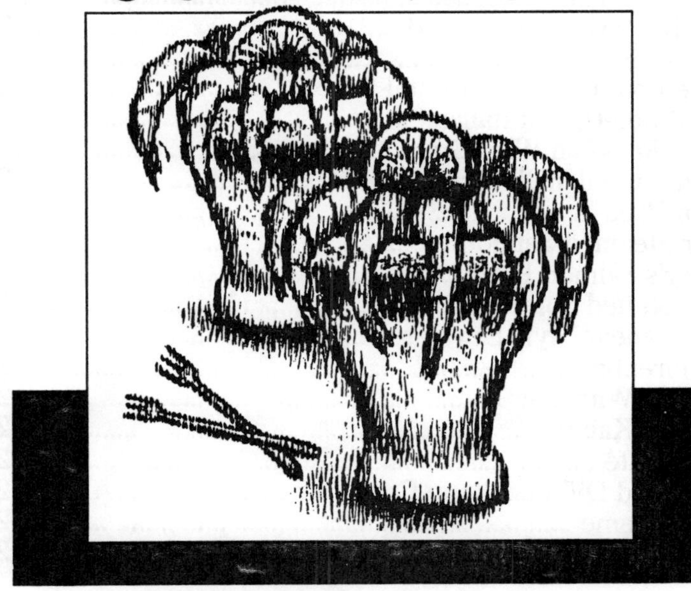

COMING: ENTERTAINING WITH SEAFOOD

CHAPTER 8

COMPANY'S COMING:
ENTERTAINING WITH SEAFOOD

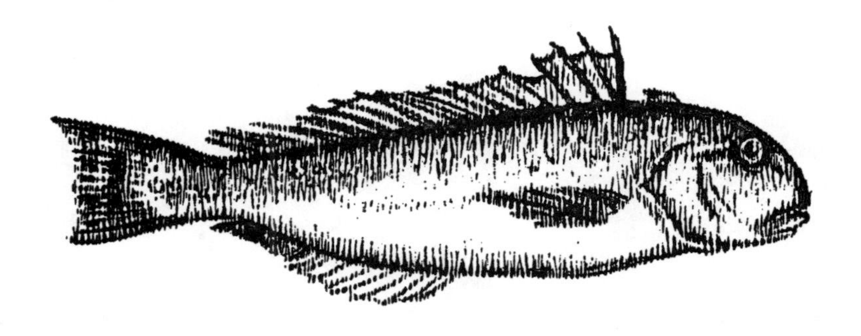

ENTERTAINING TIPS

Dining out at a seafood restaurant is an elegant experience and is one that can be easily duplicated at home. These hints will assure a successful meal for family and friends.

■ Start by becoming comfortable with ten recipes. Keep ingredients needed for these recipes on hand.

■ Invest in a special serving dish. We eat with our eyes as well as our stomachs so the more attractive the table the more enjoyable the meal.

■ Keep a supply of decorative dinner napkins or cloth napkins and candles on hand for last minute dinner parties. It is so handy to pull out these supplies, in the right color or theme, from the napkin drawer.

■ Prepare at least two dishes ahead of time. Always greet guests at the door and sit down for a hot cup of coffee or glass of wine with them.

■ Keep it simple. Elaborate menus leave no time for family and friends. Parties are not for impressing but for enjoying. When people go home, they should have enjoyed an attractive table, shared good food and interesting conversation and, most importantly, had a good time.

■ Set the table ahead of time. Having the table ready saves last minute hurry and scurry and looks inviting.

■ Add an extra course of appetizer or soup. This will stretch the meal and allow for smaller portions of the entrée.

■ If the occasion arises, let volunteering guests help with last minute preparation. People oftentimes like to help and closer relationships with family and friends can be formed at the kitchen sink. There is something special about cooking together.

GRILLED CATFISH

2 lbs. catfish fillets, skinless

Sauce:
2 tablespoons vegetable oil
⅓ cup lemon juice
¼ cup onion, chopped
2 tablespoons catsup
2 teaspoons Worcestershire sauce
4 bay leaves, crushed
2 cloves garlic, minced
¼ teaspoon pepper
2 teaspoons sugar

paprika

Place fish in a single layer in a shallow baking dish. To make sauce: combine remaining ingredients, except paprika. Pour sauce over fillets and let stand for 30 minutes, turning once. Remove fillets, reserving sauce for basting. Place fillets on lightly-oiled grill. Sprinkle with paprika. Cook about 4 inches from charcoals for 5 minutes. Baste with sauce and sprinkle with paprika. Turn and cook for 5-10 minutes longer or until fish flakes when tested with a fork. Recipe may be broiled in oven. Serve with corn on the cob and fresh fruit. Makes 8 servings.

160 calories per serving *7 grams fat per serving*
120 mg sodium per serving *60 mg cholesterol per serving*

Substitutions: *orange roughy, marlin, swordfish*

HALIBUT IN TARRAGON

"Using our recipe guidelines, we adapted this recipe from a famous Hawaiian restaurant entrée. It is wonderful for entertaining."

1½ lbs. halibut cheeks or fillets
½ cup plain low fat yogurt
1 tablespoon mayonnaise
1 teaspoon dried tarragon
¾ cup part-skim mozzarella cheese, grated

Place halibut in 8x8-inch baking pan. Mix all other ingredients together and spread over halibut. Bake at 400° for 15 minutes or until fish flakes when tested with a fork. Serve with steamed carrots and cold pasta salad. Makes 6 servings.

240 calories per serving — *8.5 grams fat per serving*
260 mg sodium per serving — *75 mg cholesterol per serving*

Substitutions: *marlin, salmon, tilefish*

Halibut cheeks have been a recognized delicacy by halibut longliners of the North Pacific halibut fishery. To this day, many of the longliners remove the cheeks from the halibut, before they deliver them to the processors, keeping the "best for themselves".

HAYMARKET HALIBUT

⅔ cup onion, thinly sliced
2 lbs. halibut fillets, boneless
1½ cups mushrooms, sliced
⅓ cup tomatoes, chopped
¼ cup green pepper, finely chopped
¼ cup parsley, minced
3 tablespoons pimiento, finely chopped
½ cup white wine
2 tablespoons lemon juice
¼ teaspoon dried dill weed
⅛ teaspoon pepper
lemon wedges

Arrange onion slices in the bottom of a lightly-oiled baking dish and place fish on top. Combine mushrooms, tomatoes, green pepper, parsley and pimiento and spread over fish. Combine wine, lemon juice, dill weed and pepper and pour over all. Cover and bake at 400° for 20 minutes or until fish flakes when tested with a fork. Serve with lemon wedges and baked potato. Makes 8 servings.

145 calories per serving *1.4 grams fat per serving*
75 mg sodium per serving *56 mg cholesterol per serving*

***Substitutions:** shark, mahi mahi, orange roughy*

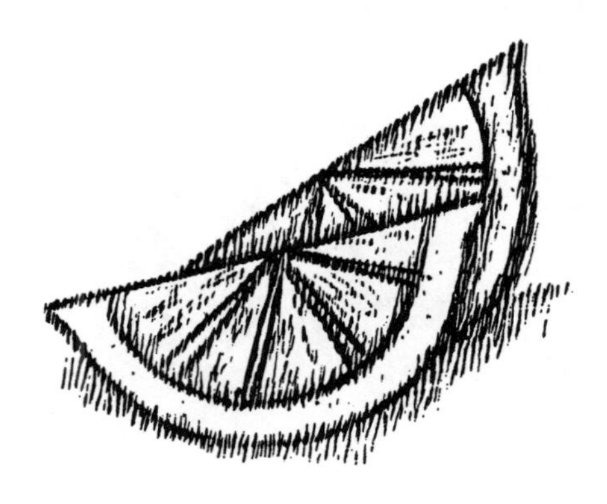

THYMELY MARINATED LINGCOD

½ cup onion, chopped
2 tablespoons vegetable oil
½ teaspoon dried thyme
½ teaspoon dried oregano
½ teaspoon dried rosemary
½ teaspoon pepper
¼ teaspoon salt (optional)
½ cup lemon juice
1 clove garlic, minced

2 lbs. lingcod fillets

Combine all ingredients in a bowl and marinate lingcod for 30 minutes. Broil or barbecue until fish flakes when tested with a fork. Makes 8 servings.

115 calories per serving 4.3 grams fat per serving
82 mg sodium per serving (calculated without salt)
90 mg cholesterol per serving

Substitutions: *cod, halibut, orange roughy*

MONKFISH FINGERS

"Poor Man's Lobster"

1½ lbs. monkfish, cut into fingers to resemble shape of lobster (approximately 2 inches by 1 inch)
½ cup flour
1 tablespoon margarine
1 tablespoon olive oil
1 clove garlic, minced
juice from ½ fresh lemon
¼ teaspoon fine herbs or bouquet garni
pepper to taste
paprika

Lightly flour monkfish fingers. Melt margarine in skillet, wok or frying pan; add olive oil, garlic, lemon juice, fine herbs and pepper. Sauté monkfish fingers for about 2 minutes or until fish flakes when tested with a fork. Remove from heat. Sprinkle with paprika. Serve with boiled potatoes and steamed vegetables. Makes 6 servings.

140 calories per serving *7.4 grams fat per serving*
45 mg sodium per serving *40 mg cholesterol per serving*

Substitutions: *squid strips, scallops, halibut cheeks*

The monkfish is an unusual-looking fish distinguished by its huge head, tooth-filled mouth and tiny eyes. This fish is also known as anglerfish, goosefish, bull mouth, devilfish and frogfish. Only the tail section is utilized as the fishermen cut off and discard the enormous head and belly section. Monkfish was named when, not too many years ago, only monks ate this fish. Its firm, white flesh and mild, sweet flavor is highly prized. It can be baked, poached, sautéed or broiled to resemble "lobster".

ORANGE ROUGHY WITH ORIENTAL SAUCE

Sauce:
¼ cup orange juice
2 tablespoons vegetable oil
2 tablespoons light soy sauce
1 tablespoon lemon juice
1 clove garlic, minced
⅛ teaspoon pepper

2 lbs. orange roughy

Combine sauce ingredients. Marinate orange roughy in sauce for 15-20 minutes. Place fish on lightly-oiled grill and barbecue over hot charcoals or broil in oven. Brush fish frequently with sauce during cooking. Cook until fish flakes when tested with a fork. Makes 8 servings.

120 calories per serving *3.8 grams fat per serving*
270 mg sodium per serving *72 mg cholesterol per serving*

Substitutions: *halibut, ocean perch, cod*

SEAFOOD ROLL-UPS IN ITALIAN SAUCE

Italian Sauce:
2 small onions, chopped
1 clove garlic, minced
2 tablespoons vegetable oil
1 - 3⅓ oz. can mushrooms, sliced
1 - 8 oz. can tomato sauce and 1 can water
¼ cup parsley, chopped
3 tablespoons lemon juice
¼ cup white wine
¼ teaspoon dried rosemary
1 teaspoon sugar

2 lbs. pollock fillets
½ cup Parmesan cheese, grated

To make Italian Sauce: sauté onion and garlic in hot oil until onion is transparent. Add mushrooms, tomato sauce, water, parsley, lemon juice, wine and seasonings; simmer about 30 minutes. Place 2 tablespoons of sauce in the middle of each fillet. Roll up like jelly rolls. Place in a shallow baking dish with the ends underneath to keep them from unrolling. Pour remaining sauce over the fish rolls. Sprinkle with Parmesan cheese. Bake at 400° for 20 minutes or until fish flakes when tested with a fork. Serve with pasta and vegetables. Makes 8 servings.

180 calories per serving *6 grams fat per serving*
360 mg sodium per serving *75 mg cholesterol per serving*

Substitutions: *sole, ocean perch, hoki*

ALASKAN ROCKFISH WITH CRAB

2 tablespoons margarine
2 lbs. rockfish (snapper) fillets
pepper to taste
½ cup onion, finely chopped
½ cup white wine
1 cup canned tomatoes, undrained
3½ oz. imitation crab

Melt margarine in a baking pan. Place rockfish in pan and sprinkle lightly with pepper. Add onion, white wine and tomatoes. Flake crab over all and bake at 400° for 15-20 minutes or until fish flakes when tested with a fork. Makes 8 servings.

135 calories per serving *3 grams fat per serving*
210 mg sodium per serving *55 mg cholesterol per serving*

***Substitutions:** cod, halibut, squid steaks*

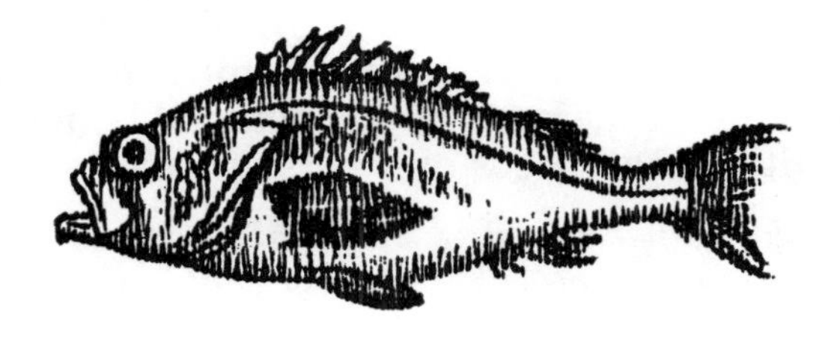

SALMON STUFFED WITH RICE

1 whole dressed salmon, about 3 lbs.
(multiply stuffing for larger salmon)

Stuffing:
2 tablespoons margarine
½ cup celery, finely chopped
¾ cup mushrooms, sliced
⅛ teaspoon dried thyme
½ teaspoon poultry seasoning
lemon pepper to taste
1½ cups water
2 tablespoons lemon juice
¾ cup uncooked rice
½ cup onion, chopped
2-3 tablespoons pimiento, diced

lemon slices
parsley

Rinse fish. Remove head and tail, if desired. Set fish aside while preparing stuffing. Heat margarine in saucepan; add celery and mushrooms and sauté about 5 minutes. Add seasonings, water and lemon juice. Bring to a boil and mix in uncooked rice. Add onion and pimiento. Cover stuffing mixture and cook on low heat for 20 minutes. Remove from heat and let stand about 5 minutes. Pat fish dry and fill cavity with stuffing. Wrap fish in foil. Place in a shallow baking pan. Bake at 400° for 30-40 minutes or until fish flakes when tested with a fork. Remove upper skin and bones if desired. Garnish with lemon slices and parsley. Makes 8 servings.

235 calories per serving *10 grams fat per serving*
100 mg sodium per serving *75 mg cholesterol per serving*

Substitutions: *whole dressed trout or mackerel*

SALMON PLAKI

2 lbs. salmon fillets, boneless
2 tablespoons olive oil
pepper to taste
1 teaspoon dried oregano
2 cloves garlic, minced
1 tomato, thinly sliced
1 onion, thinly sliced
½ cup parsley, minced
1 lemon, thinly sliced
½ cup dry bread crumbs

Place fish in lightly-oiled baking pan. Spread oil over fillets. Sprinkle with pepper, oregano and garlic. Layer with tomato slices, onion rings and parsley. Top with lemon slices and bread crumbs. Bake at 375° for 30 minutes. NOTE: You may wish to cover the dish loosely with foil halfway through baking to prevent lemons from becoming too crisp. Serve with whole grain rolls, steamed rice and fresh fruit. Makes 8 servings.

225 calories per serving *12 grams fat per serving*
10 mg sodium per serving *55 mg cholesterol per serving*

Substitutions: *bluefish, tilefish, lingcod*

Plaki is a Greek word for baked fish.

GINGER STEAMED SALMON

1 whole dressed salmon (about 3 lbs.)
1 tablespoon margarine
lemon juice
1 medium onion, thinly sliced
lemon, thinly sliced
pepper
fresh ginger, grated

Rinse fish. In fish cavity insert bits of margarine, lemon juice, onion and lemon slices. Sprinkle inside and outside with pepper and ginger. Wrap loosely in foil. Place fish on rack directly over boiling water in large pot. Cover and steam about 6-10 minutes per pound or until fish flakes when tested with a fork. Makes 6 servings.

190 calories per serving | *10 grams fat per serving*
95 mg sodium per serving | *70 mg cholesterol per serving*

Substitutions: *whole dressed mackerel, trout or rockfish (snapper)*

Invite friends over for a Chinese dinner. Serve Ginger Steamed Salmon with favorite Chinese dishes.

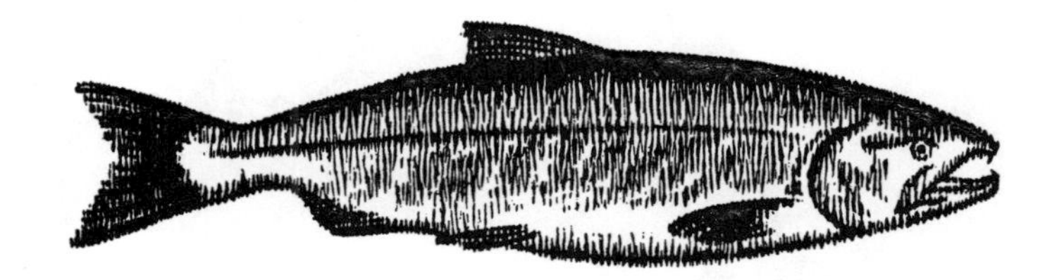

SEAFARER'S SALMON PIE

Parmesan Crust:
1½ cups flour
¼ cup Parmesan cheese, grated
⅓ cup vegetable oil
¼ cup skim milk

Filling:
1 - 15½ oz. can salmon, drained and flaked
1 large onion, finely minced
1 garlic clove, minced
½ cup green pepper, finely chopped
½ cup red pepper, finely chopped
1 cup non-fat quark or processed low fat cottage cheese
2 eggs, beaten
1 cup part-skim mozzarella cheese, grated
1 teaspoon dried dill weed
¼ teaspoon salt
1 teaspoon Worcestershire sauce

To make crust: combine flour and cheese in a bowl. In a separate bowl mix oil and milk until creamy. Pour liquid mixture over flour mixture and stir lightly with a fork until blended. Pat the dough with fingers or spoon into a 9-inch pie or quiche pan, pressing into bottom and up sides of pan. Bake at 375° for 10 minutes. Makes a 9-inch single crust. To make filling: combine all ingredients in a bowl. Pour into Parmesan Crust. Bake at 375° for 65 to 75 minutes. Cool 15 minutes. Serve with fresh fruit. Makes 8-12 servings.

235 calories per serving *11 grams fat per serving*
367 mg sodium per serving *67 mg cholesterol per serving*

SAVORY STUFFED SOLE

½ lb. cooked shrimp meat, coarsely chopped
1 cup mushrooms, sliced
¼ green pepper, chopped
¼ cup onion, chopped
1 clove garlic, minced
⅓ cup dry bread crumbs
¼ teaspoon pepper
¼ teaspoon salt (optional)
2 tablespoons fresh parsley, chopped
½ cup Farmer's cheese, grated
1 egg or 2 egg whites, slightly beaten
1½ lbs. sole fillets
½ cup dry white wine
¼ cup lemon juice
1-2 tablespoons Farmer's cheese, grated

In medium bowl, mix together shrimp, mushrooms, green pepper, onion, garlic, bread crumbs, pepper, salt, parsley and cheese. Stir in beaten egg (or whites) and mix well. Spread mixture over fillets. Roll fillets and place seam side down in a baking dish. Pour wine and lemon juice over fish. Bake uncovered at 400° for 20-30 minutes or until fish flakes when tested with a fork. While baking, occasionally baste fillets with wine and lemon mixture. During last 5-8 minutes, sprinkle fillets with additional grated cheese. Serve with pasta. Makes 6 servings.

180 calories per serving 5 grams fat per serving
330 mg sodium per serving (calculated without salt)
80 mg cholesterol per serving

Substitutions: *pollock, cod, orange roughy*

MEDITERRANEAN-STYLE SEA BASS

2 lbs. sea bass fillets, boneless
3 tablespoons margarine, melted
pepper
2 cloves garlic, minced
½ cup green onion, finely chopped
½ cup celery, finely chopped
¼ cup green pepper, finely chopped
½ teaspoon dried oregano
1 tablespoon sugar
¼ teaspoon pepper
1 - 8 oz. can tomato sauce
½ cup white wine
⅓ cup dry bread crumbs
⅓ cup Parmesan cheese, grated

Cut fish into 8 portions. Pour melted margarine in a 9x13-inch baking pan. Place fillets in pan and sprinkle with pepper. In a bowl combine garlic, onion, celery, green pepper, oregano, sugar and pepper with tomato sauce and wine. Pour on top of fillets. Sprinkle bread crumbs and cheese over top of fillets. Bake uncovered at 400° for 20-30 minutes or until fish flakes when tested with a fork and top is browned. Serve with hot rice, green salad and hot garlic bread. Makes 8 servings.

195 calories per serving *6 grams fat per serving*
400 mg sodium per serving *70 mg cholesterol per serving*

Substitutions: *rockfish (snapper), halibut, catfish*

SOLE FLORENTINE

Stuffing:
1 tablespoon margarine
½ cup mushrooms, sliced
1 - 10 oz. package frozen spinach, chopped, thawed and thoroughly drained
⅓ cup green onion, sliced
1 cup cooked rice
½ teaspoon dried dill weed
¼ teaspoon pepper

1½ lbs. sole

Sauce:
1 tablespoon margarine
2 tablespoons flour
1¼ cups skim milk
¾ cup part-skim mozzarella cheese, grated
1 teaspoon Worcestershire sauce
½ teaspoon dry mustard
dash cayenne pepper

lemon slices
parsley

To prepare stuffing: melt 1 tablespoon margarine in skillet; add mushrooms, spinach and green onion; cook until tender. Add rice, dill weed and pepper. Lay out sole fillets; divide stuffing among fillets. Roll up and fasten with toothpicks. Place in a lightly-oiled shallow baking dish. Bake at 400° for 15-20 minutes or until fish flakes when tested with a fork. To prepare sauce: in a saucepan melt 1 tablespoon margarine. Add flour and cook, stirring, until bubbly and smooth. Remove from heat and gradually blend in milk. Add remaining ingredients. Cook over moderate heat, stirring until thickened and smooth. Serve over fish. Garnish with lemon slices and parsley. Makes 6 servings.

295 calories per serving *8.7 grams fat per serving*
410 mg sodium per serving *65 mg cholesterol per serving*

Substitutions: *pollock, hoki, flounder*

SWORDFISH WITH GARLIC

"A Twenty-Minute Meal"

Seasoned Margarine:
1 tablespoon margarine
4 cloves garlic, minced
pepper to taste
2 tablespoons vermouth

2 lbs. swordfish steaks

To make seasoned margarine: melt margarine in saucepan. Add garlic and sauté until garlic begins to color. Season with pepper and add vermouth. Place fish on broiler pan and baste with seasoned margarine. Broil 4 inches from heat source for 10-15 minutes or until fish turns opaque. Baste occasionally with seasoned margarine. Makes 8 servings.

160 calories per serving — *6.5 grams fat per serving*
95 mg sodium per serving — *55 mg cholesterol per serving*

Substitutions: *shark, scallops, haddock*

SWORDFISH KABOBS

1 lb. swordfish, cut into 1-inch cubes
1 - 20 oz. can unsweetened pineapple chunks, reserve 3 tablespoons of juice

Marinade:
2 tablespoons light soy sauce
2 tablespoons sherry
2 teaspoons fresh ginger, grated
½ teaspoon dry mustard
2 cloves garlic, minced
1 teaspoon brown sugar
2 tablespoons vegetable oil

1 or 2 large green peppers, par-boiled, cut into large pieces

Place swordfish cubes in marinade pan. Drain pineapple and reserve 3 tablespoons juice. Set pineapple chunks aside. Make marinade by combining reserved juice, soy sauce, sherry, ginger, mustard, garlic, brown sugar and oil. Stir well and pour over swordfish. Cover and marinate in refrigerator for 30 minutes, turning once. Using bamboo or metal skewers, make kabobs by alternating pineapple, green pepper and swordfish; set aside. Place on lightly-oiled grill 4-5 inches from hot charcoals and cook 4-5 minutes or until swordfish turns opaque. The kabobs may be broiled in the oven. Serve with pasta salad and fresh fruit. Makes 4 servings.

300 calories per serving *11.5 grams fat per serving*
450 mg sodium per serving *50 mg cholesterol per serving*

Substitutions: *shark, halibut, monkfish medallions*

Let guests at dinner be creative and helpful by making their own kabobs.

OYSTER SAUTÉ

2 tablespoons margarine
½ cup white wine
⅓ cup celery, chopped
2 cups mushrooms, sliced
½ cup green onion, chopped
½ cup red or green pepper, chopped
1½ lbs. small oysters or 3 - 8 oz. jars small oysters
1 teaspoon dried dill weed
fresh parsley, chopped
squeeze of lemon

Sauté margarine, wine and vegetables in a saucepan until tender-crisp. Add oysters and dill weed and sauté in pan until oysters are opaque. Sprinkle with parsley and squeeze of lemon. Serve with pasta and orange slices. Makes 6 servings.

160 calories per serving *4 grams fat per serving*
350 mg sodium per serving *55 mg cholesterol per serving*

Substitutions: *scallops, peeled and deveined shrimp (prawns), croaker*

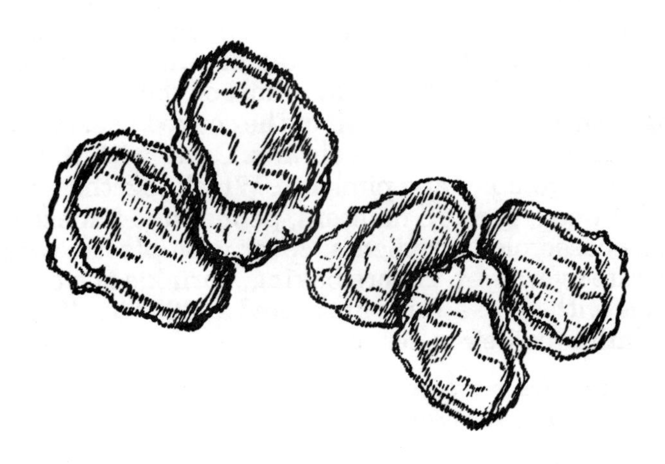

SHRIMP & DILL LUNCHEON CASSEROLE

1 teaspoon margarine
½ large green pepper, diced
1 large green onion, finely chopped
1 clove garlic, minced
7 slices French bread, cubed
1 - 2 oz. jar pimiento, drained
4 oz. cooked shrimp meat
5 eggs
1 cup skim milk
3 tablespoons fresh dill, chopped
or 1 tablespoon dried dill weed
2 tablespoons parsley, chopped
2 teaspoons Dijon mustard
¼ teaspoon pepper
¼ teaspoon hot pepper sauce (Tabasco)
3 tablespoons part-skim mozzarella cheese, grated

Spray a 9 x 13-inch baking dish with a non-stick cooking spray and set aside. Heat the margarine in a saucepan over medium heat and add the green pepper, green onion and garlic. Sauté for about 3 minutes or until vegetables are tender-crisp. Cool slightly. Place half of the bread cubes in baking dish; sprinkle with half of the cooked vegetables, half of the pimiento and all of the shrimp. Cover with the remaining bread, vegetables and pimiento. Whisk together the eggs, milk, dill weed, parsley, mustard, pepper and Tabasco. Pour over the casserole ingredients, cover with plastic wrap and refrigerate overnight. Before baking, sprinkle the top of the casserole with cheese. Bake uncovered at 325° for 40 minutes. Cool 5 minutes before serving. Makes 12 servings.

99 calories per serving *3 grams fat per serving*
137 mg sodium per serving *143 mg cholesterol per serving*

Substitutions: *imitation crab, sole fillets*

PIZZA SUPREME

12-inch cooked, thick pizza crust, such as Boboli
3 tablespoons non-fat quark
or processed low fat cottage cheese
¼ cup Marinara Sauce (see page 247)
½ cup onion, finely chopped
½ green pepper, finely chopped
1½ cups mushrooms, thinly sliced
2 tablespoons olives, finely chopped
½ lb. cooked shrimp meat
4 tablespoons part-skim mozzarella cheese, grated

Spread quark and Marinara Sauce over pizza crust. Layer onion, green pepper, mushrooms and olives over crust. Top with shrimp meat. Sprinkle cheese over all. Bake at 400° for 20 minutes. Makes 8 servings.

212 calories per serving *5 grams fat per serving*
417 mg sodium per serving *50 mg cholesterol per serving*

Substitutions: *crab meat, anchovies, imitation crab*

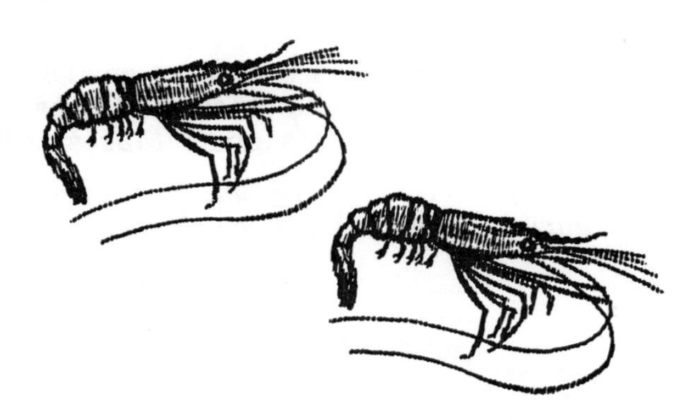

SUPERB STUFFED SQUID (CALAMARI)

1¼ lbs. whole squid

Stuffing:
¾ cup part-skim mozzarella cheese, grated
2 tablespoons parsley, chopped
1 teaspoon dried oregano
1 teaspoon dried basil
⅓ cup Parmesan cheese
½ cup dry bread crumbs
⅓ cup onion, finely chopped
1 cup mushrooms, chopped

2 cups Marinara Sauce (see page 247)
2 tablespoons Parmesan cheese, grated
¼ cup part-skim mozzarella cheese, grated, for topping

Clean squid, keeping mantles (bodies) whole. To make stuffing: combine cheese, parsley, oregano, basil and Parmesan cheese; mix well. Stir in bread crumbs, onion and mushrooms. Stuff squid until plump, but not packed. Close opening and secure with toothpick. Pour small amount of Marinara Sauce into 11x7-inch glass or ceramic baking dish. Arrange squid in single layer in baking dish. Top with Marinara Sauce and 2 tablespoons Parmesan cheese. Bake uncovered at 350° for 20 minutes. Top with mozzarella cheese and bake an additional 10 minutes or until squid is tender. Makes 4 servings.

250 calories per serving — *5 grams fat per serving*
470 mg sodium per serving — *270 mg cholesterol per serving*

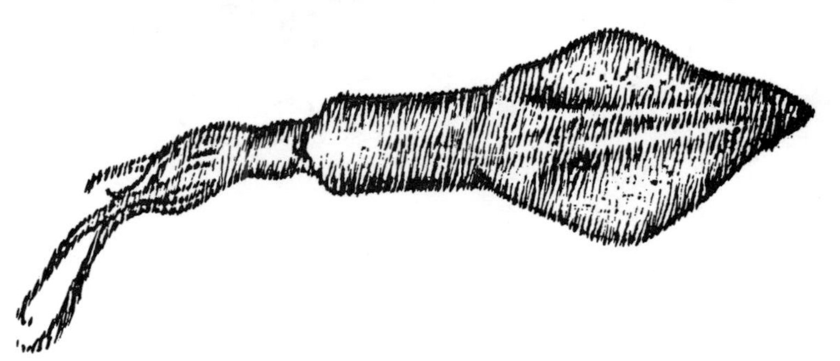

C H A P T E R   N I N E

ROMANTIC

DINNERS

FOR TWO

CHAPTER 9

ROMANTIC DINNERS FOR TWO

SAUTÉED ORANGE ROUGHY

2 teaspoons margarine
½ cup white wine
½ teaspoon dried dill weed
1 garlic clove, minced
¼ cup mushrooms, chopped
½ lb. orange roughy
parsley, chopped
lemon wedges

Heat margarine, wine, dill weed, garlic and mushrooms in skillet until hot. Add fish; sauté until fish flakes when tested with a fork. Remove to a warm platter. Sprinkle with parsley. Garnish with lemon wedges. Makes 2 servings.

160 calories per serving *4 grams fat per serving*
125 mg sodium per serving *67 mg cholesterol per serving*

Substitutions: *cod, flounder, lingcod*

Orange roughy is imported from New Zealand. Its name comes from its brilliantly orange skin. However the fillets are white and have a delicate flavor.

TERIYAKI SABLEFISH (BLACK COD)

Marinade:
1 tablespoon light soy sauce
2 tablespoons sherry
1 clove garlic, minced
½ teaspoon fresh ginger, grated or
¼ teaspoon ground ginger
1 teaspoon honey

½ lb. sablefish (black cod) steaks
lemon wedges

To make marinade: combine soy sauce, sherry, garlic, ginger and honey. Marinate sablefish in soy marinade about 30 minutes, turning once. Broil 4 inches from heat source about 10-15 minutes or until fish flakes when tested with a fork. Garnish with lemon wedges. Serve with rice. Makes 2 servings.

165 calories per serving *5.6 grams fat per serving*
450 mg sodium per serving *65 mg cholesterol per serving*

Substitutions: *salmon, sturgeon, shark*

SWEETHEARTS' SALMON SAUTÉ

"A fifteen-minute meal"

1 tablespoon margarine
¼ cup white wine
¼ cup mushrooms, sliced
8 oz. salmon fillets or steaks
lemon
fresh parsley, chopped

Heat margarine, wine and mushrooms in a sauté pan or skillet until hot. Place salmon in pan; sauté until done. Squeeze lemon over fish. Sprinkle with parsley before serving. Serve with pasta and steamed peas. Makes 2 servings.

225 calories per serving *13 grams fat per serving*
120 mg sodium per serving *75 mg cholesterol per serving*

Substitutions: *sole, flounder, ocean perch*

All 5 species of salmon are equally nutritious but vary in color, texture and cost.

Sockeye (red) — ***is firm in texture and deep red in color. Next to the King it is the most expensive salmon.***

Pink — ***is your best buy. It is most often canned and has a fine texture with color ranging from light peach to deep pink.***

Coho (silver) — ***is pink-fleshed and has a fine texture. It is a moderately priced salmon.***

King (Chinook) — ***is the most prized salmon. The King is the largest salmon and has a softer flesh that ranges from deep red to almost white. It is rich in oil.***

Chum (Keta) — ***has coarse texture and the palest color. It is less expensive than other varieties and is an economical choice.***

SOLE PRIMAVERA IN A SHELL

"For A Special Meal"

Marinade:
10 button-sized mushrooms, sliced
2 green onions, chopped
½ cup celery, diced
½ cup carrots, coarsely grated
⅔ cup broccoli flowerets, chopped
⅔ cup white wine

¾ teaspoon bouquet garni
¾ teaspoon lemon peel, finely grated
2 teaspoons dried parsley
2 cloves garlic, minced
¼ teaspoon pepper
3 tablespoons margarine
6 sheets filo dough
8 ozs. sole, thinly sliced
½ cup flour
1 tablespoon Parmesan cheese, grated
1 tablespoon part-skim mozzarella cheese, grated

In a covered 1-quart bowl marinate mushrooms, onion, celery, carrots and broccoli in white wine overnight. In a non-stick saucepan, simmer marinade and vegetables with bouquet garni, lemon peel, parsley, garlic and pepper until tender or about 6 minutes over medium heat. Drain the cooked vegetables and set aside.

In a small pan melt margarine. On a large board or flat surface, sparingly brush one sheet of filo dough with the melted margarine. Place the second sheet of filo dough on top of the first sheet and brush sparingly with margarine. Repeat the process with the third sheet of filo dough.

Lightly flour half of sole. Place the floured sole parallel to one edge in the center of the layers of filo dough. Place half well-drained, cooked vegetables on top of sole. Mix cheeses together. Sprinkle vegetables with half cheese mixture. Fold ends of filo dough to the middle overlapping one edge of dough layers by about ½-1 inch. Brush margarine sparingly over seam. Carefully roll the seafood and filo, beginning at the end containing fish. Brush margarine sparingly over the entire roll-up. Repeat process for second serving. Bake at 350° for 30 minutes. Makes 2 servings.

615 calories per serving *18 grams fat per serving*
370 mg sodium per serving *60 mg cholesterol per serving*

***Substitutions:** flounder, salmon, cod*

CRAB ST. JACQUES

½ cup mushrooms, sliced
2 tablespoons onion, finely minced
1 tablespoon margarine
2 teaspoons cornstarch
½ cup skim milk
1 tablespoon dry white wine
1 tablespoon lemon juice
¼ teaspoon dried thyme
⅛ teaspoon white pepper
8 oz. crab meat
dry bread crumbs
1 oz. part-skim mozzarella cheese, grated

Sauté mushrooms and onion in margarine. Blend in cornstarch. Add milk, wine and lemon juice. Cook on medium heat, stirring constantly, until thickened and smooth. Blend in seasonings. Add crab and heat through. Divide between 2 scallop shells or individual au gratin dishes. Sprinkle bread crumbs and mozzarella cheese over casseroles. Broil 3-4 minutes or until lightly browned. Serve with fruit plate and whole wheat roll. Makes 2 servings.

280 calories per serving *10 grams fat per serving*
410 mg sodium per serving *80 mg cholesterol per serving*

Substitutions: *imitation crab, scallops, cooked shrimp meat*

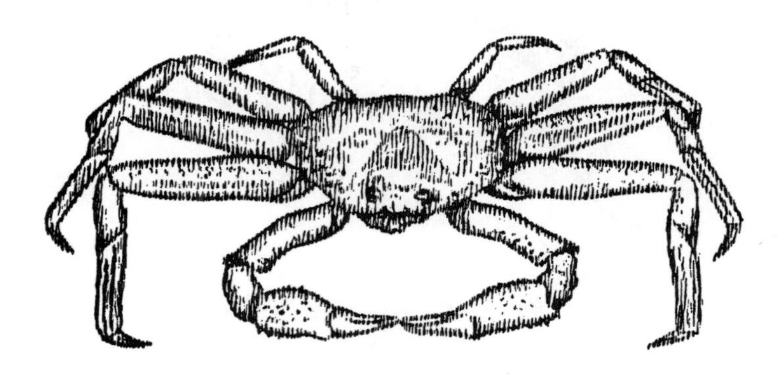

LOVERS' LOBSTER TAILS

1 lb. lobster tails (7 to 8 oz. each)
1 tablespoon margarine, melted
1 clove garlic, minced

MICROWAVE METHOD:
Split each lobster tail through top shell and release meat, leaving it connected to shell at one end. Pull meat through slit and place on top of shell. Arrange tails in baking dish and brush with margarine and garlic. Cover with plastic wrap. Microwave 3 minutes on HIGH or until meat is opaque and shell turns red. This recipe is also delicious sautéed. Overcooking causes meat to toughen. Makes 2 servings.

150 calories per serving *9 grams fat per serving*
280 mg sodium per serving *90 mg cholesterol per serving*

Substitution: *large shrimp (prawns) in shell*

All of the lobster is edible except for the bony shell structure, the small crop or craw in the head of the lobster, and the dark vein running down the back of the body meat.

A fresh lobster varies from shades of green or brown to occasionally deep blue. The bright red color of the lobster is obtained only by cooking.

Cook a lobster by dropping it head first into a pot of lightly salted boiling water. When the water starts to boil again, allow ten minutes for a 1-pound lobster and two to three minutes for each additional pound.

Have a beach party by using seawater to cook the lobster. This gives an excellent flavor to the meat.

SCALLOP SAUTÉ WITH ALMONDS AND GRAPES

½ lb. scallops
2 teaspoons margarine
¼ cup onion, finely chopped
1 teaspoon brown sugar
1 teaspoon Dijon mustard
2 tablespoons white wine
½ cup fresh grapes, seedless
2 tablespoons slivered almonds
lemon wedges
parsley, chopped

Sauté scallops with onion in margarine about 2 minutes. Add brown sugar, mustard, wine and grapes. Toss until onion is tender-crisp, grapes are heated through and all ingredients are nicely coated with pan sauce and scallops are opaque. Do not overcook. Serve sprinkled with slivered almonds; garnish with lemon wedges and parsley. Serve immediately. Makes 2 servings.

225 calories per serving | *8.8 grams fat per serving*
250 mg sodium per serving | *60 mg cholesterol per serving*

Substitutions: *shrimp (prawns), peeled and deveined, monkfish medallions*

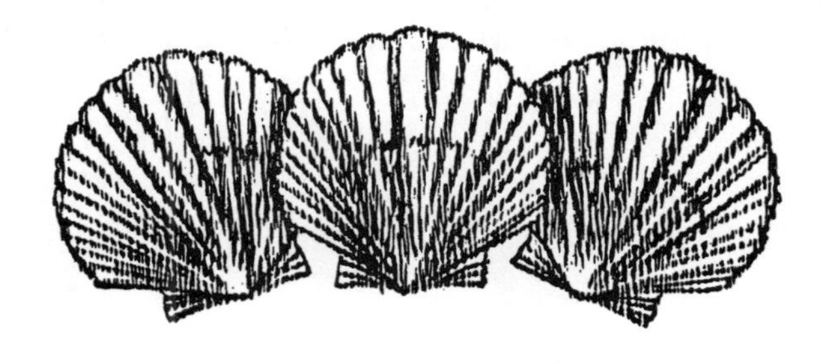

SESAME PRAWNS

"Wonderful"

1 tablespoon margarine
1 tablespoon light soy sauce
½ lb. prawns (shrimp), peeled and deveined
1 tablespoon sesame seeds
¼ cup green onion, diagonally sliced
¼ teaspoon ground ginger or
1 teaspoon fresh ginger, grated

Heat margarine in frying pan or wok. Mix soy sauce, prawns (shrimp), sesame seeds, onion and ginger. Marinate for 15 minutes. Cook over medium heat until shellfish is pink, approximately 2-3 minutes. Serve over wild rice. Makes 2 servings.

195 calories per serving *10 grams fat per serving*
515 mg sodium per serving *160 mg cholesterol per serving*

Substitutions: *squid strips, halibut cubes*

There are numerous varieties of shrimp or prawns. Size ranges from 3 to 160 shrimp or prawns to the pound. The interchange in names "shrimp" or "prawn" has no universal standard. However, in commercial practice in the U.S., prawn is used as a name for large shrimp.

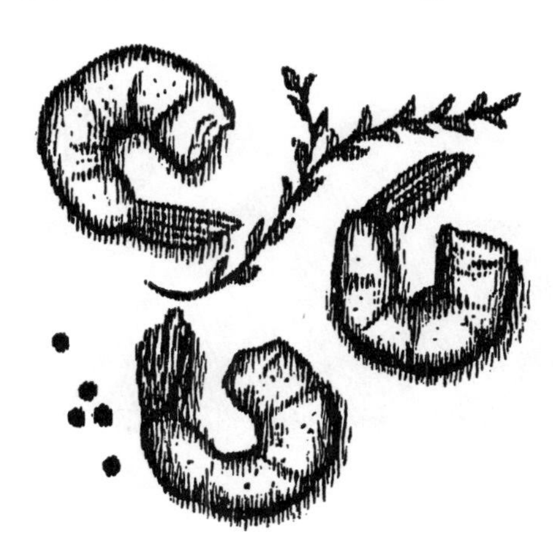

PARADISE PRAWN SAUTÉ

"A Light Meal For Two"

¼ cup unsweetened pineapple juice (drained from can)
1 tablespoon light soy sauce
¼ teaspoon fresh ginger, grated
1 tablespoon cold water
1 teaspoon cornstarch
½ lb. prawns, peeled and deveined
½ cup unsweetened pineapple chunks, drained
½ cup peas
1 stalk celery, diagonally sliced
1 green onion, chopped

Combine in saucepan, pineapple juice, soy sauce, ginger, cold water and cornstarch; bring to a boil. Reduce heat and stir until thick and clear. Add prawns, pineapple, peas, celery and green onion and sauté for 5 minutes or until thoroughly heated and prawns turn opaque; stir frequently. Serve over rice. Makes 2 servings.

200 calories per serving *1.5 grams fat per serving*
635 mg sodium per serving *160 mg cholesterol per serving*

Substitutions: *shrimp, peeled and deveined, halibut, squid strips*

CHAPTER TEN

SAUCES, DRESSINGS & DIPS

CHAPTER 10

SAUCES, DRESSINGS AND DIPS

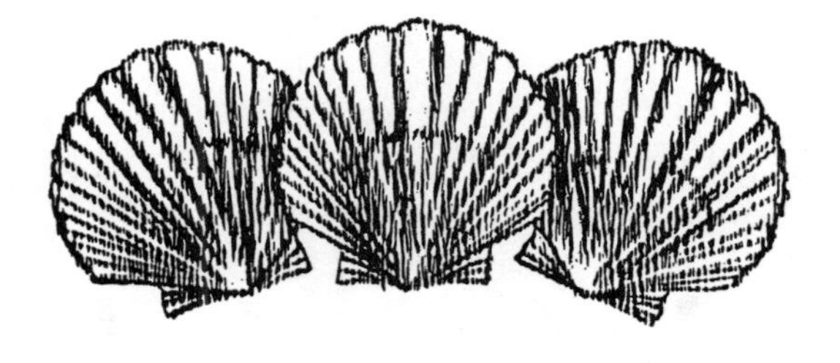

ZESTY COCKTAIL SAUCE

"Excellent for shrimp cocktail"

1 - 8 oz. can tomato sauce
2 tablespoons chili sauce
¼ teaspoon garlic powder
dash dried oregano
¼ teaspoon hot pepper sauce (Tabasco)
¼ teaspoon dried thyme
⅛ teaspoon sugar
dash dried basil

Combine all ingredients in a small saucepan. Simmer 10-12 minutes, stirring occasionally. Serve hot or cold. Excellent as a cocktail sauce on shrimp or crab appetizer. Use as a sauce for poached fish. Makes about 1 cup sauce.

8 calories per tablespoon
0 gram fat per tablespoon
110 mg sodium per tablespoon
0 mg cholesterol per tablespoon

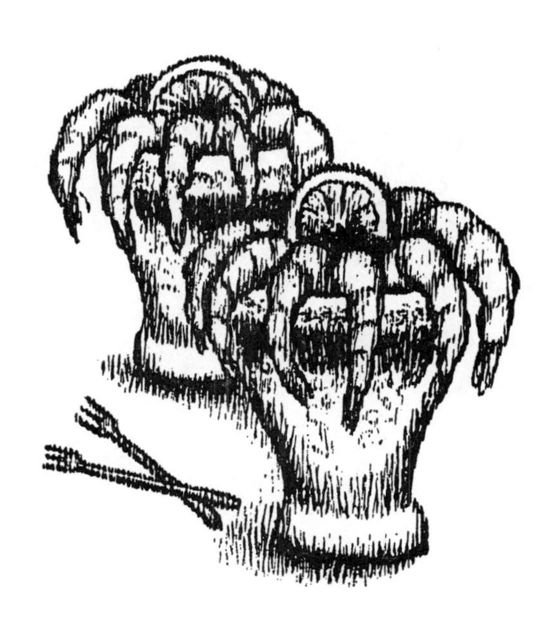

SKINNY-DIP TARTAR SAUCE

¾ cup low fat cottage cheese
¼ cup plain low fat yogurt
1 tablespoon onion, chopped
2 tablespoons cucumber, grated
1 tablespoon fresh parsley, minced
1 teaspoon celery flakes

Blend cottage cheese in blender until smooth. Mix cottage cheese with all other ingredients in a bowl and refrigerate. Makes 1 cup.

12 calories per tablespoon *.2 gram fat per tablespoon*
25 mg sodium per tablespoon *1 mg cholesterol per tablespoon*

HEART-HEALTHY SEAFOOD DIP

8 oz. plain low fat yogurt
½ cup cucumber, diced
½ cup celery, diced
½ cup carrot, shredded
1 tablespoon onion, finely chopped
½ teaspoon paprika
1 tablespoon Worcestershire sauce
1 teaspoon lemon juice

In a medium bowl, combine all ingredients; mix well. Cover and chill for one hour. Use as a tartar sauce for seafood or as a dip for raw vegetables such as mushrooms, celery, or carrot sticks. Makes 1¾ cups or 28 - 1 tablespoon servings.

7.6 calories per serving *.1 gram fat per serving*
7 mg sodium per serving *.4 mg cholesterol per serving*

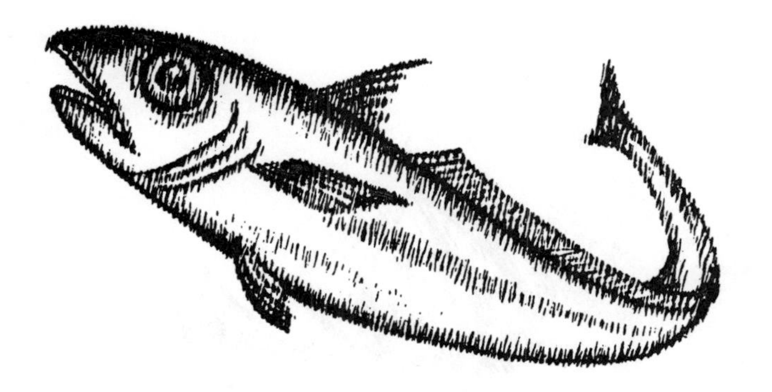

SNAPPY BARBECUE SAUCE

¼ cup onion, finely chopped
2 cloves garlic, minced
1 tablespoon vegetable oil
1 - 8 oz. can tomato sauce
½ cup unsweetened applesauce
2 tablespoons cider vinegar
⅛ teaspoon cayenne pepper

In saucepan, sauté onion and garlic in oil until tender. Add remaining ingredients and simmer 15 minutes. Serve sauce over barbecued fish or barbecued oysters. Leftover sauce freezes well. Enjoy barbecued fish on French bread using Snappy Barbecue Sauce as a topping. Makes 8 - 2½ tablespoon servings.

30 calories per serving *1.8 grams fat per serving*
170 mg sodium per serving *0 mg cholesterol per serving*

BARBECUE BASTING SAUCE

2 tablespoons margarine
½ teaspoon dried dill weed
¼ teaspoon onion powder
1 tablespoon lemon juice
⅛ teaspoon pepper

Melt margarine. Add remaining ingredients. Brush on barbecued fish during the last 2-3 minutes of cooking or pour over barbecued oysters (see page 171) before serving. Makes 4 servings.

50 calories per serving *7 grams fat per serving*
70 mg sodium per serving *0 mg cholesterol per serving*

RATATOUILLE PROVENÇALE

4 tomatoes, diced
½ lb. eggplant, diced
1 onion, chopped
1 clove garlic, minced
1 cup white wine or vermouth
1 teaspoon dried basil
½ teaspoon pepper
dried oregano to taste

Sauté tomatoes, eggplant, onion and garlic. Allow the tomatoes to cook down until almost a sauce. Stir in the wine. Add basil, pepper and oregano. Allow to simmer 10 minutes. Serve with poached fish on a bed of rice. Makes 4 servings.

95 calories per serving *.5 gram fat per serving*
5 mg sodium per serving *0 mg cholesterol per serving*

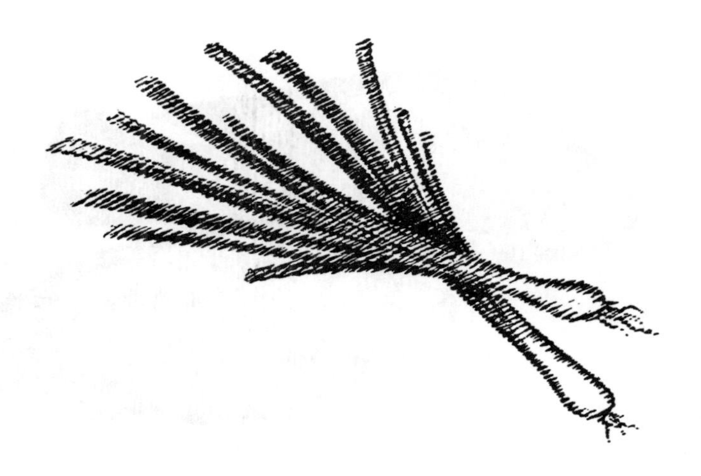

ITALIAN SAUCE

1 tablespoon vegetable oil
1 cup tomato sauce
3 tablespoons white wine
juice of 1 lemon
1 tablespoon wine vinegar
2 cloves garlic, minced
1 teaspoon dried oregano
1 teaspoon dried mint
2 bay leaves, crushed

Heat oil in skillet or saucepan over moderate heat. Combine remaining ingredients and cook, uncovered, over low heat for 15-20 minutes until slightly thickened. Pour over steamed fish just before serving or serve in a separate sauceboat. Makes 1¼ cups.

40 calories per serving — *2.8 grams fat per serving*
260 mg sodium per serving — *0 mg cholesterol per serving*

BASIC WHITE SAUCE

1 tablespoon margarine
1 tablespoon flour
white pepper
1 cup skim milk
¼ teaspoon salt

Melt margarine in a saucepan over low heat. Blend in the flour and pepper to make a roux. Cook on low heat, stirring, until the mixture is smooth and bubbly. Stir in the milk and salt. Heat to boiling and cook 1 minute, stirring constantly. For medium-thick white sauce: increase margarine and flour to 2 tablespoons each. Makes 1 cup. Serve over poached or steamed fish.

Basic sauce:

50 calories per serving — *3 grams fat per serving*
210 mg sodium per serving — *0 mg cholesterol per serving*

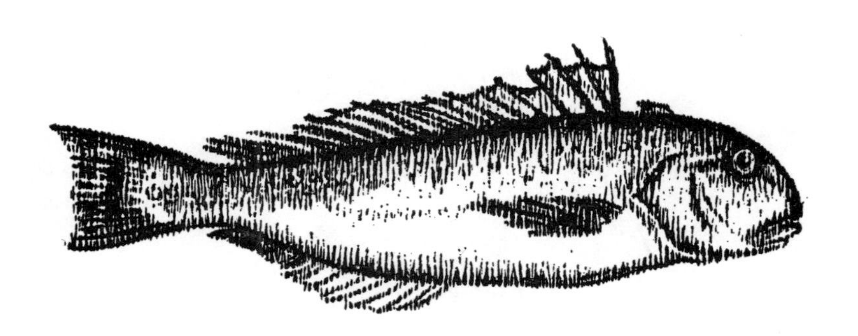

CAPER SAUCE

1 cup plain low fat yogurt
2 tablespoons capers, chopped
1 tablespoon lemon juice
1 tablespoon parsley, chopped
2 teaspoons dried instant minced onion
1 teaspoon lemon rind, grated

Combine all ingredients and mix thoroughly. Chill several hours or overnight. Serve with poached fish. Makes 4 servings.

50 calories per serving *.8 gram fat per serving*
90 mg sodium per serving *5 mg cholesterol per serving*

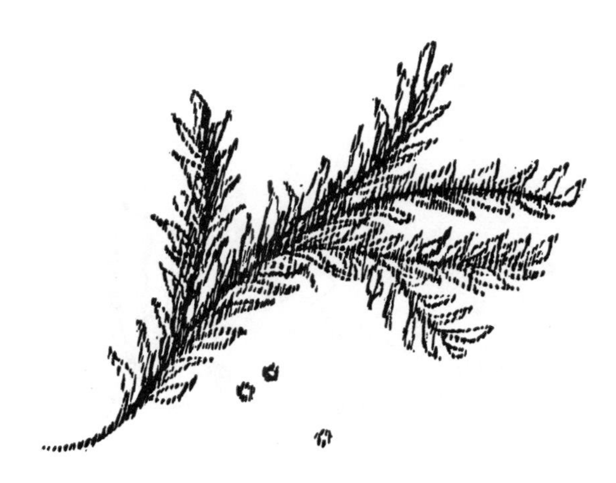

LEMON RELISH

¼ cup parsley, chopped
½ cup green onion, chopped
¼ cup fresh lemon juice

Combine all ingredients in a bowl. Use as an excellent complement to broiled, steamed or sautéed fillets. Makes 1 cup.

3 calories per tablespoon *0 gram fat per tablespoon*
0 mg sodium per tablespoon *0 mg cholesterol per tablespoon*

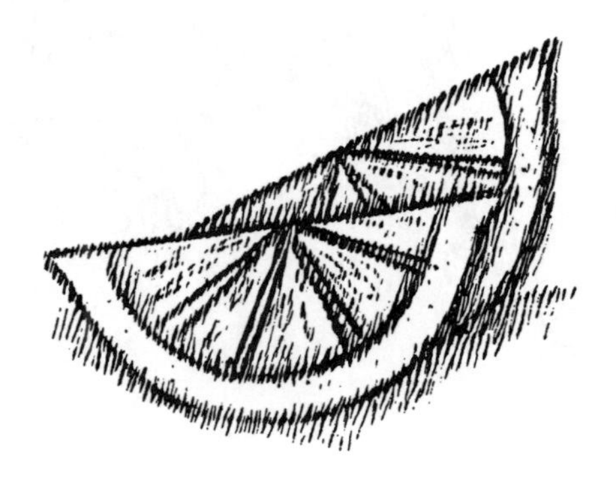

THOUSAND ISLAND DRESSING

1 cup low fat cottage cheese
¼ cup chili sauce
¼ cup plus 2 tablespoons skim milk
1 teaspoon paprika
2 tablespoons celery, finely chopped
2 tablespoons green pepper, finely chopped
2 tablespoons ripe black olives, finely chopped
1 tablespoon sweet pickle relish
1 tablespoon onion, finely chopped
1 tablespoon Parmesan cheese, grated

Combine first 4 ingredients in food processor; process until smooth. Stir in remaining ingredients. Chill. Makes 2 cups.

10 calories per tablespoon
30 mg sodium per tablespoon
1.8 grams fat per tablespoon
1 mg cholesterol per tablespoon

SWEDISH CREAM SAUCE

1 cup low fat cottage cheese
¼ cup cucumber, grated
2 tablespoons chives, chopped

Mix ingredients together and chill. Serve with poached or steamed fish. Makes 1¼ cups sauce or 4 servings.

55 calories per serving · *1 gram fat per serving*
120 mg sodium per serving · *5 mg cholesterol per serving*

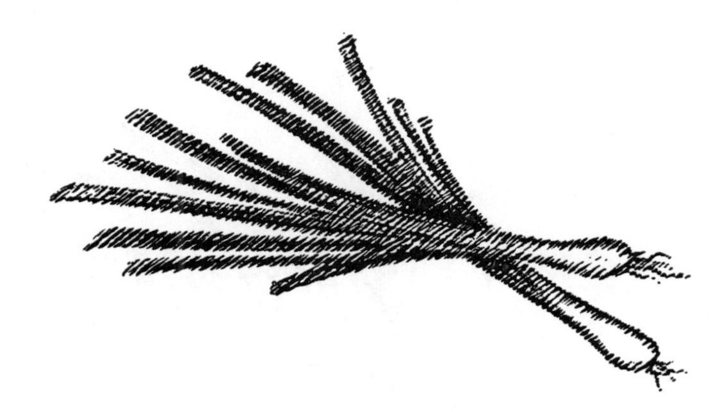

MARINARA SAUCE

1 tablespoon olive oil
4 cloves garlic, chopped
1 cup onion, chopped
1 cup mushrooms, chopped
1 - 28 oz. can whole tomatoes, undrained
½ teaspoon dried oregano
½ teaspoon dried basil
¼ teaspoon pepper
½ teaspoon sugar

In large skillet, heat olive oil. Add garlic, onion, and mushrooms and sauté until just tender. Stir in remaining ingredients, breaking up tomatoes with spoon. Cook over medium heat until sauce thickens, approximately 30 minutes. Serve over hot pasta or cooked seafood. Makes about 3 cups sauce or 4 servings.

90 calories per serving | *4 grams fat per serving*
268 mg sodium per serving | *0 mg cholesterol per serving*

SALSA

2 medium tomatoes, coarsely chopped
¼ cup red onion, chopped
3 tablespoons green chiles, diced
2-3 dashes hot pepper sauce (Tabasco)

Combine all ingredients and blend well. Let stand at room temperature or in refrigerator for 15-20 minutes to blend flavors. Makes about 1¼ cups sauce or 4 servings.

20 calories per serving *0 gram fat per serving*
2 mg sodium per serving *0 mg cholesterol per serving*

CHAPTER ELEVEN

GENERAL INFORMATION

CHAPTER 11

GENERAL INFORMATION

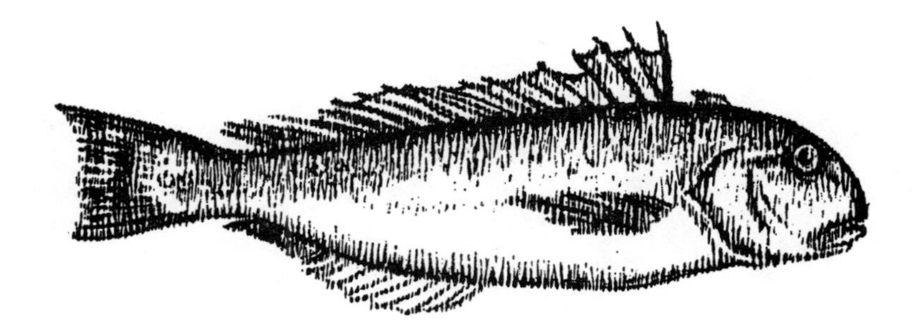

BIBLIOGRAPHY

Adams, C.: *Nutritive Value of American Foods in Common Units,* Agriculture Handbook No. 456, USDA, U.S. Government Printing Office, Washington D.C., 1975.

Kromhout, D., Bosschieter, E. and Coulander, C.: *The Inverse Relation Between Fish Consumption and 20-Year Mortality From Coronary Heart Disease.* The New England Journal of Medicine, May 9, 1985: 312: 1205-09.

Pennington, J. and Church, H.: *Food Values of Portions Commonly Used,* Bowes and Church (13th edition). Harper & Row, New York, 1980.

Research Dept. of the National Live Stock and Meat Board, *Nutrient Values of Muscle Foods – Composition Values for Specific Cuts of Meat, Poultry and Fish.* Edition One, Chicago, IL, 1988.

Sidwell, V.: *Chemical and Nutritional Composition of Finfishes, Whales, Crustaceans, Mollusks, and Their Products.* U.S. Dept. of Service, Springfield, VA, 1981.

USDA, Human Nutrition Information Service, *Composition of Foods: Finfish and Shellfish Products.* U.S. Dept. of Commerce, NOAA, NMFS, National Technical Information Service, Springfield, VA, 1985.

USDA, *Provisional Table HNIS/PT-103.* 1985.

US DHHS: National Institute of Health, *Facts About Blood Cholesterol*. National Heart, Lung, and Blood Institute, Bethesda, MD, 1987, 88-2696.

ABOUT THE AUTHORS

As food educators, cookbook authors, award-winning gourmet cooks, and nutrition and marketing consultants, Janis Harsila and Evie Hansen have become the nation's leading ambassadors of seafood education.

Janis, a registered dietitian, and Evie, an experienced marketing professional, combined their special knowledge, expertise and experience to form National Seafood Educators–Nutrition Division. This unique consulting firm provides practical information about seafood to media, retailers, health professionals and consumers. Through their two best-selling cookbooks and their overflow demonstration workshops, these seafood educators offer nutrition facts and cooking tips to help make preparing seafood healthful and convenient.

In 1990, Janis Harsila was honored as the Washington State Young Dietitian of the Year, and holds membership in the American Dietetic Association. She is an authoritative resource for health care professionals and consumers alike about the latest research linking seafood balanced diets with positive health benefits.

Evie Hansen appeared in the *Who's Who in Business and Finance* and *Who's Who in the West*. She studied education at Seattle Pacific University, received a Seafood Quality Control Certificate from the University of Washington, and completed a seafood merchandising program at Oregon State University.

From the beginning, National Seafood Educators has pioneered the development of seafood and health awareness programs. "Seafood is Heart Food", their program co-sponsored by the American Heart Association, was the first nationwide seafood consumer awareness campaign. In 1986, National Seafood Educators published the first edition of *Seafood: A Collection of Heart-Healthy Recipes,* followed by *Light-Hearted Seafood* in 1989. Both best-selling books are recommended by most major health organizations (American Dietetic Association, etc.) and have earned rave reviews.

Janis and Evie are not only seafood nutrition, cooking and marketing authorities, but they practice what they teach. Both have lived for many years on Puget Sound in Washington State, one of the most diverse, seafood-rich areas in the nation. In addition, the two seafood educators grew up in families that relied on the sea's harvest, married husbands who are successful Pacific Northwest commercial fishermen, and now have their own growing families who regularly enjoy seafood.

ORDERING INFORMATION

Please send me _____ copies of *Seafood: A Collection of Heart-Healthy Recipes*

@$13.95 each

or 3 copies .... @$36.95 $ ________

Also available:

Please send me ______ copies of *Light-Hearted Seafood*

@ $10.95 each

or 3 copies .... @ $29.95 $ ________

Shipping and Handling

$2.00 1st book, each additional book add $1.00. $ ________

Washington residents add sales tax:

$1.13 per *Seafood: A Collection of Heart-Healthy Recipes* ($2.99 per 3 copies)

$ .89 per *Light-Hearted Seafood* ($2.43 per 3 copies) $ ________

TOTAL ENCLOSED $ ________

I enclosed ☐ Check ☐ Money Order

Bill my ☐ VISA ☐ MASTERCARD

Card # ________________________ Expires ____________

Phone________________________

Ship to:

Name ____

Address ____

City ______________________ State ______ Zip __________

Mail payment to:
National Seafood Educators
P.O. Box 60006
Richmond Beach, WA 98160
Phone: (206) 546-6410
FAX: (206) 546-6411

Seafood: A Collection of Heart-Healthy Recipes - ISBN 0-9616426-2-9
Light-Hearted Seafood - ISBN 0-9616426-1-0

DIABETIC EXCHANGES

	Pg.	Bread	MEAT			Veg.	Fruit	MILK			Fat	
RECIPE	#		lean	med.	high			skim	low	whole		COMMENTS
After Work Grouper (Chilean Sea Bass)	186		3			1						
Alaskan Rockfish With Crab	207		3									
Almond Shrimp (Prawns) And Peppers	178		3			1						
Autumn Fish Stew	94	1	3			1						
Baked Tilapia Fillets With Oregano	156	1	3 1/2									
Barbecue Basting Sauce	239										1	
Barbecued Oysters In The Shell	171		1									
Barbecued Salmon	140		3									
Basic White Sauce	242					1					1	
Basil Baked Cod	117		3									
Bayside Rockfish	138		3									
Broiled Salmon Steaks With Herb Sauce	142		3								1	
Broiled Scallop Sauterne	173		2 1/2									
Cantonese-Style Lingcod	189	1/2	3									
Caper Sauce	243							1/2				
Catfish Ettouffée	115	1/2	3									
Chopped Seafood Salad	80			2		1						
Citrus-Baked Haddock	187		3				1/2					
Clams Mozzarella	164	1	4									
Corn Chowder	98	2	1					1			1	
Crab Broccoli Casserole	167	1	1 1/2									

RECIPE	Pg. #	Bread	MEAT			Veg.	Fruit	MILK			Fat	COMMENTS
			lean	med.	high			skim	low	whole		
Crab Louie	75		3									
Crab St. Jacques	228	1	3½									
Crab Stuffed Mushrooms	61	½	1			1						
Crab With Red Sauce	168		3									
Crispy Baked Flounder	119	½	2									
Croaker Stir-Fry	118	1	3									
Cucumber Tuna Spread	71		2									
Curry Tuna Salad	89		1				1					
Danish Sandwiches	106	1		1								
Easy Shrimp And Pea Salad	83	½	1									
English Muffin Shrimp Pizza	102	1	1									
Everybody's Mackerel	127		3									
Fettucine With Salmon	145	2	2			1						
Fisherman's Choice Oysters	172		2½									
Five-Spice Haddock	121		3									
Garden Fresh Coleslaw	84		1			1						
Ginger Steamed Salmon	210		3			½						
Gingered Shrimp (Prawns) On Skewers	179		3									
Grilled Catfish	200		3									
Grilled Halibut Mexicana	125	½	3									
Grilled Shark Teriyaki	148		4				2					
Halibut In Tarragon	201		3½									

	Pg.	Bread	MEAT			Veg.	Fruit	MILK			Fat	
RECIPE	**#**		**lean**	**med.**	**high**			**skim**	**low**	**whole**		**COMMENTS**
Halibut On A Bed Of Vegetables	188		3			4						
Halibut Vegetable Chowder	95	1/2	3									
Haymarket Halibut	202		3			1						
Heart-Healthy Seafood Dip	237											Free: 3 tablespoons
Hoki Sauté	126	1/2	3									
Holiday Fish Spread	69		1									per 3 appetizers
Hot Crab Spread	59		1					1/2				per 5 tablespoons
Hot Seafood Salad	76	1/2	2									
Huke Lodge Breakfast Trout	158			4 1/2			1/2					
Hurry Up Baked Pollock	133	1/2	3									
Island Fresh Cucumber Salad	82		1			2						
Italian Cioppino	93	1/2	2									
Italian Flounder Roll-ups	120	1/2	3									
Italian Sauce	241					1						
Judy's Tuna Puffs	72	1/2		1								
Layered Seafood Salad	81		3			1						
Lemon Baked Rockfish	135		3			1						
Lemon Broiled Ocean Perch	130		3									
Lemon Relish	244											Free: 1/4 cup serving
Lemon-Herbed Sole	153		3									
Linguini With Clam Sauce	163		2			1						sauce only
Lively Crab Dip	60	1/2	1/2									per 6 tablespoons

	Pg.	Bread	MEAT			Veg.	Fruit	MILK			Fat	
RECIPE	#		lean	med.	high			skim	low	whole		**COMMENTS**
Lobster Roll	101	½	1½									
Lovers' Lobster Tails	229		3									
Lunchbreak Tuna Sandwich	103	1	2								1	
Macadamia Baked Mahi Mahi	128	½	3									
Marinara Sauce	247	1									1	1 cup serving
Marinated Oriental Squid (Calamari)	66	1	1									
Maryland Crab Cakes	165	1	1½									
Maui Salmon	88		1								1	
Mediterranean-Style Sea Bass	213	½	3			1						
Mexican-Style Rockfish	134		3			1						
Mickey's Favorite Oysters	194	1½	2									
Microwave Shrimp (Prawns)	195		2½									
Monkfish Fingers	204	½	3									
Monkfish With Oriental Sauce	129		3									
Monterey Squid (Calamari) Salad	86	½	2									
Mussels In Tomato Sauce	169	½	1			2						
New England Clam Chowder	97	2	2					1				
Northwest Broiled Shrimp (Prawns)	175		3									
Old-Fashioned Stuffed Haddock	122	½	3									
Opening-Day Trout	192			4							1	
Orange Roughy Under Orange Sauce	131		2									
Orange Roughy With Oriental Sauce	205		3									

	Pg.	Bread	MEAT			Veg.	Fruit	MILK			Fat	
RECIPE	#		lean	med.	high			skim	low	whole		COMMENTS
Oriental Halibut Sauté	123		3									
Oriental Stir-Fry	112	½	3			1						
Oven-Fried Halibut	124	½	3									
Oven-Poached Albacore Tuna	113		3			1						
Oven-Poached Rockfish	136		3½									
Oyster Sauté	217	½	2									
Oyster Stew	99	1	3									
Oysters On The Half Shell With Red Wine Vinegar Sauce	64		1									
Paradise Prawn Sauté	232	1	3				1½					
Parmesan Catfish	114		3									
Picante Seafood Salad	79	2	2									
Pizza Supreme	219	1½		1		1						
Poached Cod With Herbs	116		3			1						
Poached Shrimp (Prawns)	176		3									
Portuguese Skate Wings	150	½	3									
Ratatouille Provençale	240	1										
Rockfish With Lemon-Tarragon Sauce	137		3									
Salmon Curry Pilaf	146	1	2								1	
Salmon In Pita Bread	107	1½	2									
Salmon In Potato Shells	147	1	2									
Salmon Mousse	70		2									
Salmon Plaki	209	½	3								1	

	Pg.	Bread	MEAT			Veg.	Fruit	MILK			Fat	
RECIPE	**#**		**lean**	**med.**	**high**			**skim**	**low**	**whole**		**COMMENTS**
Salmon Stuffed Seashells	67	1½	4									per 4 appetizers
Salmon Stuffed With Rice	208	½	4									
Salmon Teriyaki	144	½	3									
Salmon With Cucumber Sauce	190		3			1					1	
Salmonburgers	105	½	3									
Salsa	248					1						
San Francisco-Style Shark	149	½	3									
Saturday Night Seafood Chowder	96	1	2					½				
Sautéed Orange Roughy	223		3									
Savory Stuffed Sole	212	½	3									
Scallop Sauté	174	½	2									
Scallop Sauté With Almonds And Grapes	230		2				1				1	
Scandinavian Salmon Steaks With Spinach	143	1	3								1	
Seafarer's Salmon Pie	211	1	1						1		1	
Seafood Pear Salad	77		1				1					
Seafood Roll-Ups In Italian Sauce	206		3			1						
Sesame Prawns	231		3									
Sesame Sablefish (Black Cod)	139	½	3									
Seviche	62		2									
Shrimp And Dill Luncheon Casserole	218	½	1									
Shrimp And Spinach Salad With Sunshine Dressing	78			1		2	1					
Shrimp (Prawns) In Beer	177		3									

	Pg.	Bread	MEAT			Veg.	Fruit	MILK			Fat	
RECIPE	#		lean	med.	high			skim	low	whole		COMMENTS
Shrimp Stuffed Celery	63		1			1						
Shrimp Stuffed Tomato	85	½	2									
Simply Baked Salmon	141		3									
Skewered Scallops	65		1 ½									per 2 kabobs
Skinny-Dip Tartar Sauce	236											Free: ¼ cup serving
Smokey Salmon Paté	68			1								per 3 appetizers
Snappy Barbecue Sauce	238					1						
Sole Amandine	151		3									
Sole Fillets Tarragon	152		3			1						
Sole Florentine	214	1	3									
Sole Primavera In A Shell	226	3		3							3	
Spanish-Style Cod	184	½	3									
Speedy Poached Flounder	185		3									
Spicy Grilled Orange Roughy	132		2									
Spring Salad	87		2			1					1	
Steamed Bluefish With Orange Sauce	183		3									
Steamed Mussels Or Clams	170	½	2									
Stir-Fried Squid (Calamari)	180	½	3									
Stir-Fry Swordfish And Vegetables	155	½	3			1						
Stuffed Jumbo Shrimp (Scampi)	196	1	3									
Superb Stuffed Squid (Calamari)	220	1½	3									
Swedish Cream Sauce	246		1									

	Pg.	Bread	MEAT			Veg.	Fruit	MILK			Fat	
RECIPE	**#**		**lean**	**med.**	**high**			**skim**	**low**	**whole**		**COMMENTS**
Sweet Potato Crab Cakes	166		3			2						
Sweethearts' Salmon Sauté	225		3								1	
Swordfish Kabobs	216		3				2				1	
Swordfish Steaks With Peppercorns	154		3									
Swordfish With Basil	191		3									
Swordfish With Garlic	215		3									
Take-Me-Along Seafood Sandwich	104	1	1½									
Teriyaki Sablefish (Black Cod)	224		3			1						
Thousand Island Dressing	245											Free: ¼ cup serving
Three-Minute Steamed Clams	193		3									
Thymely Marinated Lingcod	203		3									
Tilefish With Curry-Yogurt Sauce	157		3									
Tuna Chow Mein	159	1	2								1	
Unbelievably Good Squid Soup	100		1			1		1				
Zesty Cocktail Sauce	235					1						per ¼ cup serving Free: 2 tablespoons

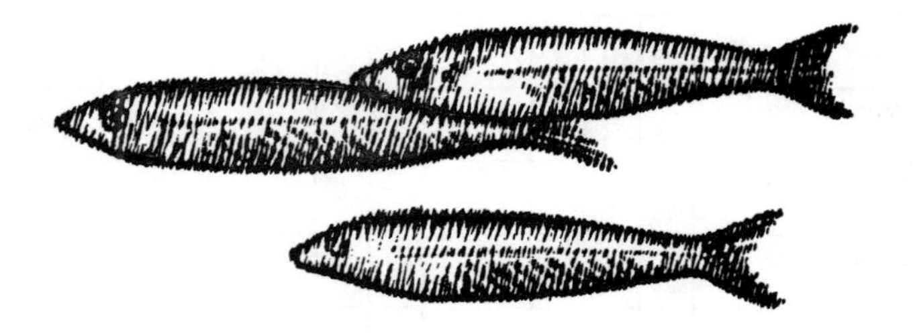

INDEX BY TITLE

J, K, L

M

N

O

P, Q, R

S

T, U

V, W, X, Y, Z

INDEX

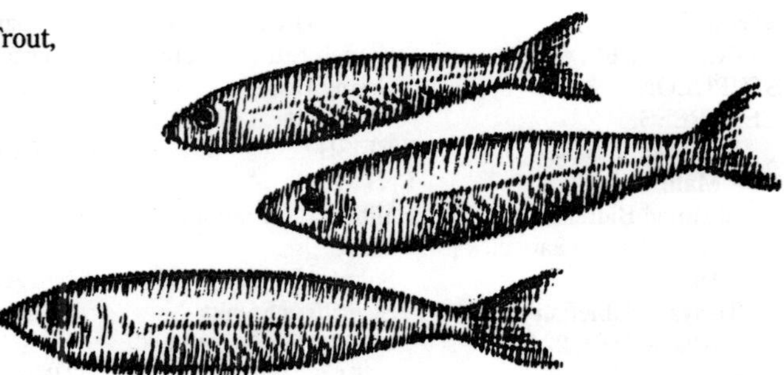